The Battle of Kursk

A Captivating Guide to One of the Largest and Most Decisive Battles of World War II

© Copyright 2024 - All rights reserved.

The content contained within this book may not be reproduced, duplicated, or transmitted without direct written permission from the author or the publisher.

Under no circumstances will any blame or legal responsibility be held against the publisher, or author, for any damages, reparation, or monetary loss due to the information contained within this book, either directly or indirectly.

Legal Notice:

This book is copyright protected. It is only for personal use. You cannot amend, distribute, sell, use, quote, or paraphrase any part, or the content within this book, without the consent of the author or publisher.

Disclaimer Notice:

Please note the information contained within this document is for educational and entertainment purposes only. All effort has been executed to present accurate, up-to-date, reliable, and complete information. No warranties of any kind are declared or implied. Readers acknowledge that the author is not engaging in the rendering of legal, financial, medical, or professional advice. The content within this book has been derived from various sources. Please consult a licensed professional before attempting any techniques outlined in this book.

By reading this document, the reader agrees that under no circumstances is the author responsible for any losses, direct or indirect, that are incurred as a result of the use of the information contained within this document, including, but not limited to, errors, omissions, or inaccuracies.

Free Bonus from Captivating History (Available for a Limited time)

Hi History Lovers!

Now you have a chance to join our exclusive history list so you can get your first history ebook for free as well as discounts and a potential to get more history books for free!

Simply visit the link below to join.

Or, Scan the QR code!

captivatinghistory.com/ebook

Also, make sure to follow us on Facebook, X, and YouTube by searching for Captivating History.

Table of Contents

INTRODUCTION 1
CHAPTER 1 – BACKGROUND TO HITLER'S WAR ON RUSSIA 3
CHAPTER 2 – BARBAROSSA, MOSCOW, AND STALINGRAD 7
CHAPTER 3 – SPRING 1943: KHARKOV AND THE PLANNING FOR KURSK 16
CHAPTER 4 – THE BATTLEFIELD AND THE OPPONENTS 26
CHAPTER 5 – THE ATTACK STARTS IN THE NORTH 41
CHAPTER 6 – THE ATTACK ON THE SOUTHERN FLANK 53
CHAPTER 7 – PROKHOROVKA: THE GREATEST EVER TANK BATTLE? 65
CHAPTER 8 – HITLER WAVERS, AND THE SOVIETS COUNTERATTACK 79
CHAPTER 9 – AFTERMATH 83
CONCLUSION 87
HERE'S ANOTHER BOOK BY CAPTIVATING HISTORY THAT YOU MIGHT LIKE 91
FREE BONUS FROM CAPTIVATING HISTORY (AVAILABLE FOR A LIMITED TIME) 92
REFERENCE 93
IMAGE SOURCES 95

Introduction

The war between Nazi Germany and communist Russia lasted four years and was a titanic and brutal struggle involving millions of soldiers and tens of thousands of tanks, aircraft, and artillery. In 1941, the German Army, which was divided into three army groups, thrust deep into the Soviet Union. They used the tried and tested application of "blitzkrieg" warfare, which involved an effective combination of troops, artillery, aircraft, mechanized armored personnel carriers, engineers, and, of course, tanks. For the first two years of this campaign, the Germans did very well. They advanced rapidly and captured millions of poorly trained Soviet soldiers. The Germans knocked out or shot down thousands of Soviet tanks and aircraft.

In 1941, Hitler promised his generals that a few short but powerful blows would be sufficient to topple Stalin and the communist regime. In the high summer of 1942, as German panzer divisions approached the Volga in the east and the Caucasus Mountains in the south, it seemed as if Hitler could still be right.

But as they moved forward, the German war machine started to wear out. Despite success after success, the Soviet Union did not collapse. It actually continued to resist the German forces, throwing increasing numbers of soldiers into the fight. After enduring one vicious Russian winter and in the midst of a second, an entire German force found itself fighting desperately in the streets of Stalingrad. A well-planned and executed series of Soviet counterattacks encircled the Germans in the city. In February 1943, the Nazis received the earth-shattering news of the German surrender at Stalingrad. Most historians see Stalingrad as the key turning point of the war in Russia and also of the Second World War in general.

Although the Germans had been defeated and pushed back hundreds of miles, they managed to counterattack and inflict heavy losses on the Soviets in and around Kharkov (now known as Kharkiv). There was still a lot of fight in the German Army, and troops, guns, and equipment—including brand-new heavy tanks—were rushed to the front to replenish and rearm the troops. The German Army's morale was high, and their divisions were the best equipped they had been in a long time. The spring and summer held the prospect of another German blitzkrieg. In the summer of 1943, no army on earth had ever stopped a blitzkrieg dead in its tracks.

This is the story of the last major German strategic offensive of the Second World War. It focuses on the key rail and road hub at Kursk. This is a tale of two battles, one north and one south of Kursk. The Germans risked everything in a gamble to cut off and eliminate the "bulge" at Kursk—a bulge that contained two million Soviet soldiers.

Could the blitzkrieg be made to work one more time?

Chapter 1 – Background to Hitler's War on Russia

A World War Begins...

On September 1st, 1939, German infantry, aircraft, and tank – or panzer – divisions launched a powerful and unprovoked assault on Poland. This heralded the start of the Second World War in Europe. Highly mobile, well-armed, and well-armored mechanized German forces surged confidently across the borders. The Wehrmacht (the German Army) employed rapid movement and hammer blows from tanks, artillery, and dive bombers. They punched holes in the Polish front lines. Once a gap had been opened, they pushed their mechanized forces quickly through, reaching deep behind the enemy's positions and fanning out into their rear. It was a technique that relied upon initiative and confidence on all levels, from generals down to the lowest of private soldiers. This move would soon be dubbed "blitzkrieg" or "lightning war." The German panzer divisions and dive bombers outmatched a brave but largely out-classed Polish army.

On September 17th, forces of the Soviet Union invaded Poland from the east in a secret pact agreed between Adolf Hitler and Joseph Stalin. The Poles were overwhelmed and powerless. Warsaw was pounded by German bombers in a grim demonstration of what was to happen across Europe for the next five years. The last organized fighting by the Polish forces took place on October 6th, barely five weeks after the invasion had begun. The Polish government surrendered, and Poland was effectively partitioned between the Nazis and the Soviets.

Britain and France reluctantly declared war on Germany as soon as the invasion of Poland began. Hitler's forces paused to regain their breath and focused westward. For some months, the war on the Western Front was stagnant. Many Western Europeans called it the "Phoney War" and hoped that the issue might be resolved without significant fighting. It was not long before the Germans struck. In April 1940, Denmark and Norway were knocked out of the war in lightning strikes by German land, air, and naval power.

However, the campaign in Scandinavia was a relatively small-scale operation: Denmark surrendered after only six hours. On May 10th, the full might of the German Army was unleashed on Holland, Belgium, Luxembourg, and France. France was one of the great powers. The French armed forces were ranked amongst the best in the world. It had powerful and numerous equipment, including roughly 3,500 tanks. The Germans had 2,500 tanks. A small but skilled British expeditionary force was also in France for support. Surely, the Germans would meet their match there.

British, French, and German generals were all too aware of the four years of blood, mud, and stagnation in the trenches in France during the First World War. Many of them had fought there. There was a concern about the potential level of bloodshed and a long, drawn-out campaign. No one, not even Hitler and his senior generals, expected what followed.

The campaign in the west lasted a mere six weeks. The rapid speed of the German mechanized forces again took their opponents by surprise. A conventional thrust by German forces into Holland and Belgium drew a large part of the Anglo-French force into Belgium to meet the Germans. At this point, a concentrated force of three German panzer corps drove through the Ardennes Forest in Luxembourg to the south and began to head straight for the English Channel.

Rooted in a defensive mentality, where ponderous plan succeeded ponderous plan, the French generals responsible for the defense of France were paralyzed. They were powerless to respond rapidly enough to the changing situation. After all, the last war lasted four years. The French headquarters, in castles or bunkers miles back in the rear, often did not have radios and were dependent on motorcyclists to relay messages amid roads crammed with terrified refugees. By the time the

French had come up with an order to maneuver their divisions, the swift German panzer divisions had already moved well beyond the intended battlefield and were even closer to the French coast and achieving their goal of splitting the Allied army in half.

The French resistance collapsed. There was no strategic French reserve of forces, which a frustrated and appalled Winston Churchill found out. Generals were seen to weep tears of frustration at the inability of their forces to respond to the speed of the German advance. The British managed a massive evacuation from Dunkirk and salvaged more than 300,000 soldiers—the foundation of an entire army that could at least defend England. It was the one glimmer of hope from a catastrophe. But as Winston Churchill pragmatically noted in that gloomy June of 1940, "We must be very careful not to assign to this deliverance the attributes of a victory. Wars are not won by evacuations."[i]

By the middle of 1940, the world had been introduced to the idea of blitzkrieg—a war conducted at such a rapid pace as to prevent the enemy from being able to react. The concept of the "panzer division" had become a byword for German military superiority and skill. It was a perfect fusion of tanks, infantry, artillery, and engineers all coming together. They were capable of operating at the same speed and adapting quickly to the rapidly evolving needs of the battlefield. They had become a psychological weapon every bit as much as a military tool. Many of the panzer generals had already become famous for their drive. Erwin Rommel and Heinz Guderian always led from the front in small armored radio vehicles.

Britain stood alone for the rest of the year. The people were fearful that Germany would launch an invasion. The Battle of Britain, the contest between the British Royal Air Force (RAF) and the German Luftwaffe in the skies over the English Channel and the fields of Kent, started almost as soon as the Battle of France had ended. The newly conquered French and Belgian ports began to fill up with invasion barges. An amphibious assault on the southern coastline of England, dubbed "Operation Sealion" by the Germans, started to look increasingly likely.

---

[i] 'Fight Them on the Beaches,' International Churchill Society, website accessed 7 June 2024, https://winstonchurchill.org/resources/speeches/1940-the-finest-hour/fight-them-on-the-beaches/

However, the Luftwaffe suffered grievous losses at the hands of the young pilots of the multi-national RAF. In reality, Hitler's desire to conquer Britain was half-hearted at best. He expressed admiration for the British Empire and hoped to come to terms that would allow Britain to keep its empire as long as Hitler could control Europe. Furthermore, Germany, as a continental presence, had no experience in large-scale amphibious operations. The invasion of Britain never happened, and it remains one of the greatest "what ifs" of military history. Hitler's writings, speeches, and thoughts—the ideology that had shaped, motivated, and propelled Nazism for over a decade—had been consistently building up to one ultimate territorial destiny.

In December 1940, Hitler ordered his generals to prepare for Operation Barbarossa, the invasion of the Soviet Union. Following in the wake of several other historic and failed attempts to invade Russia, Hitler was about to put his panzer divisions to the ultimate test and achieve what the former French emperor, Napoleon Bonaparte, had been unable to do. The panzer divisions were to play key parts in this invasion.[i]

Adolf Hitler, looking at the results achieved in Poland, the Low Countries, and France by his panzer divisions, was supremely confident in the capabilities of his armies and his own skills as a strategic military commander. He viewed the conquest of Russia as inevitable.

"We only have to kick in the door and the whole rotten structure will come crashing down."[ii]

He would be proved wrong.

---

[i] Carell, P., Hitler's War on Russia, (Harrap Ltd: London, 1987), pp19-20.
[ii] Beevor, A., *The Second World War*, (Weidenfeld and Nicolson: London, 2012), p.190.

Chapter 2 – Barbarossa, Moscow, and Stalingrad

"The hands of the carefully synchronised watches jumped to 0315. As though a switch had been thrown a gigantic flash of lightning rent the night. Guns of all calibres simultaneously belched fire. The tracks of tracer shells streaked across the sky. As far as the eye could see the front on the Bug was a sea of flames and flashes. A moment later the deep thunder of the guns swept the tower of Volka Dobrynska like a steamroller. The whine of the mortar batteries mingled eerily with the rumble of the guns. Beyond the Bug a sea of fire and smoke was raging. The narrow sickle of the moon was hidden by a wall of cloud."[i]

In the early pre-dawn hours of Sunday, June 22nd, 1941, Operation Barbarossa began. The front stretched eight hundred miles, from the Baltic Sea coastline in Poland south to Romania and the Black Sea. Three million soldiers, supported by thousands of tanks, aircraft, and artillery pieces, surged into the Soviet Union.

Stalin was not unaware of Germany's intentions—spies and allies had been reporting a German attack for months—but he had been trying to avoid provoking Hitler and giving him a *casus belli* (an act that would justify war). A trade agreement between Germany and the Soviet Union meant that Russian trains, full of raw materials for Hitler's war machine, were still clanking into Germany on the night before Operation

---

[i] Carell, P., *Hitler's War on Russia*, (Harrap Ltd: London, 1987), p21.

Barbarossa began.

Most of the Soviet troops on the border had been specifically ordered not to man their forward positions in order to avoid confrontations. As a result, the Soviet forces were entirely unprepared. The border crossings and key bridges were seized almost without resistance. Hundreds of Soviet aircraft were caught. They were lined up on the ground and destroyed.

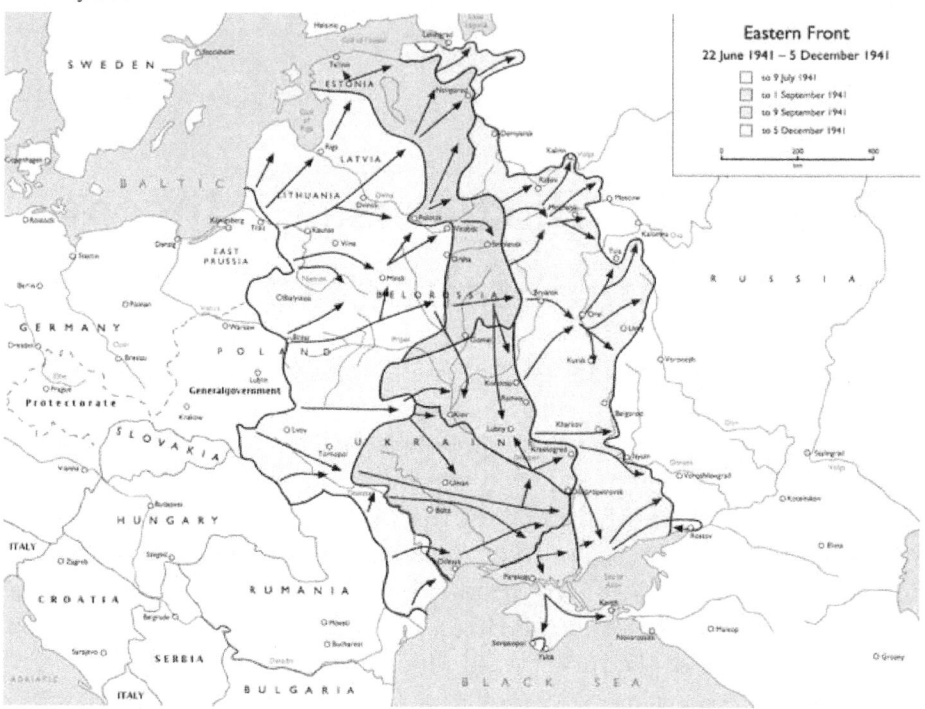

There were spectacular gains for the German Army in the first six months of the campaign in Russia.[1]

The German attack was divided into three army groupings, each with its own allotted panzer and infantry divisions. They were supported by dedicated Luftwaffe fleets. Army Group North sought to capture the Baltic states and then head northeast to take Leningrad. Army Group Center—the most powerful of the groups—was pointed at Smolensk and, ultimately, Moscow. Army Group South dived into Ukraine, the "bread basket" of the Soviet Union. This region was full of grain and mineral resources that would greatly aid the army or nation that controlled it.

The lessons of the Polish and French campaigns had demonstrated that tanks worked best if concentrated into a tight armored fist to punch through and exploit gaps in an enemy front line. During Operation Barbarossa, the German commanders did exactly that. The panzer divisions were concentrated into large panzer armies, one per army group.

Those first few months brought staggering success to the fast-moving panzer and motorized divisions at the front of the German advance. They sliced through confused and poorly trained Soviet soldiers with ease, advancing hundreds of miles into Soviet territory and encircling tens—and sometimes even hundreds—of thousands of Soviet soldiers. The Germans struggled to cope with the volume of prisoners they took. In October, at Vyazma, just over 130 miles west of Moscow, 600,000 Soviet prisoners were marched into captivity and to a highly uncertain but generally fatal fate as slave laborers.

The panzers pressed ever deeper into western Russia. The newspaper headlines in Germany and around the world told of the great distances traveled and the large numbers of prisoners taken. Yet, problems were emerging in the German Army. Poorly trained, poorly equipped, and poorly led Soviet soldiers could be easily defeated, particularly if they were outflanked and surrounded. However, they also fought savagely to the death if aided by good defensive positions. Furthermore, not all the Soviet military equipment was of low quality. The Soviet tanks came as a shock to the German soldiers. The T-34 was a rugged and highly mobile modern machine with sloped armor that could deflect anti-tank shells and a potent 76.2 mm anti-tank gun. German tanks, at best, had anti-tank guns of a 50 mm caliber. The Soviet KV-1 also had a 76.2 mm gun and had even thicker armor than the T-34—90 mm at the front and 75 mm on the sides. By comparison, the heaviest German tank at the time, the Panzerkampfwagen ("Panzer" or Pz.) Mark IV, that crossed into Russia for Operation Barbarossa could only boast 50 mm armor on the front and 30 mm on the sides.

The German anti-tank gun, the Panzerabwehrkanone (Pak), which was issued as standard to the infantry divisions, was a small and light weapon with a shell caliber of 37 mm. It had been effective enough against Polish, French, and British armor in 1939 and 1940, but it was almost entirely inadequate against a T-34. It gained the derisory nickname of "door knocker" by the German soldiers who witnessed the shells strike and bounce off Soviet tanks without causing any damage.

After encountering the T-34 and KV-1 on the battlefield, the German armaments industry scrambled to upgrade the armor and armaments of existing tanks and also commenced the urgent development of new tanks, two of which, the Pz. V "Panther" and the Pz. VI "Tiger," would be intricately involved in the Battle of Kursk in 1943.

General Heinz Guderian noted that 145 German divisions were available for Operation Barbarossa. Of these, only nineteen were full-fledged panzer divisions capable of highly mobile activities. Most of the German infantry divisions were still required to march on foot in the wake of the fast-moving panzers and relied on horses to pull their supplies, artillery, and other equipment. Wherever there was a crisis or a need for urgent action, it was always the panzer divisions that were called upon.

As a result, the German panzer formations suffered from extensive wear and tear, which was exacerbated by the blistering heat of the summer, the thick mud of the autumn, and the frosts, snow, and sub-zero temperatures as winter began to set in. The tanks traveled hundreds of miles, which extended their supply chains. Spare parts and fuel took much longer to be moved along the dusty, bumpy dirt tracks that passed for highways in western Russia. Russian infrastructure was poor, and roads and rail networks were limited. In France, the German tank crews advanced on tarmac roads and could pull up at a French petrol station and fill their fuel tanks. This was not an option in the vast expanse of the Soviet Union. It also seemed that Soviet land, manpower, and equipment reserves were endless; even though many soldiers were defeated, many more came behind them.

In December 1941, Hitler had a discussion with General Heinz Guderian regarding the Russian numerical superiority in tanks and the urgent need for replacements for the German tanks. During the exchange, Hitler reportedly retorted in exasperation, "If I had known that the figures for Russian tank strength [ten thousand] which you gave in your book were in fact the true ones, I would not have started this war."[i]

Nevertheless, by December 1941, the gains of the Wehrmacht were impressive. Some units had traveled six hundred miles. In the north, the crucial city port of Leningrad was under siege, and in the south, most of

---

[i] Guderian, H., *Panzer Leader,* (Futura: London, 1980), p.190.

Ukraine had been overrun. Army Group Center was tantalizingly within binocular range of the suburbs of Moscow.

However, the Soviet army regrouped and recovered to some extent. Reinforcements were rushed over from Siberia; Stalin understood that Japan would be attacking America, not Russia. The winter weather was severe for the Germans. Most soldiers were still in their summer uniforms, and winter gear, including both equipment and clothing, was limited. To keep the panzers mobile, fires had to be started underneath the tank engines every morning in order to warm them up before the engine could be started.

German advances slowed to a crawl. At this low ebb of the Wehrmacht in Russia, powerful Soviet counterattacks orchestrated by one of Stalin's most experienced commanders, Georgy Zhukov, struck into the flanks of the German troops outside of Moscow. The Germans were thrown back in disarray, abandoning weapons and equipment. Moscow had been saved, and the Russians learned that the Germans were beatable.

The savage winter conditions prohibited further movement, and the spring thaw in March generated another carpet of mud that hampered operations. As the ground began to firm up, both sides prepared for the coming campaigning season. At Stalin's insistence (and against the advice of some of his generals), the Red Army launched an offensive around Kharkov on May 12th. It was commanded by Marshal Timoshenko. The attack was premature; the Soviet forces were not yet ready. They were unable to undertake such complex operations. The Russians suffered massive casualties, and the advance was stopped by German ground forces and the power of the Luftwaffe after just three days. A well-organized German counterattack (Operation Fredericus, also known as the Second Battle of Kharkov) followed days later and lasted into mid-June. Three Soviet armies were cut off, amounting to about a quarter of a million men who were either killed or captured. It was a major defeat for the Russians and a personal humiliation for Stalin.

By the end of June, it was time for the Germans to take the offensive. Stalin was expecting that the Germans would have another go at taking Moscow, having gotten so close the previous year. However, that summer, Hitler turned his attention to the southeast and the Caucasus, where extensive oilfields held the prospect of a permanent solution to German worries about fuel shortages. Italian, Hungarian, and Romanian divisions formed part of Operation Blue. German morale began to improve, as infantry and panzer divisions were filled again with replacement soldiers. New tanks, guns, and aircraft arrived to bring the formations back up to combat readiness.

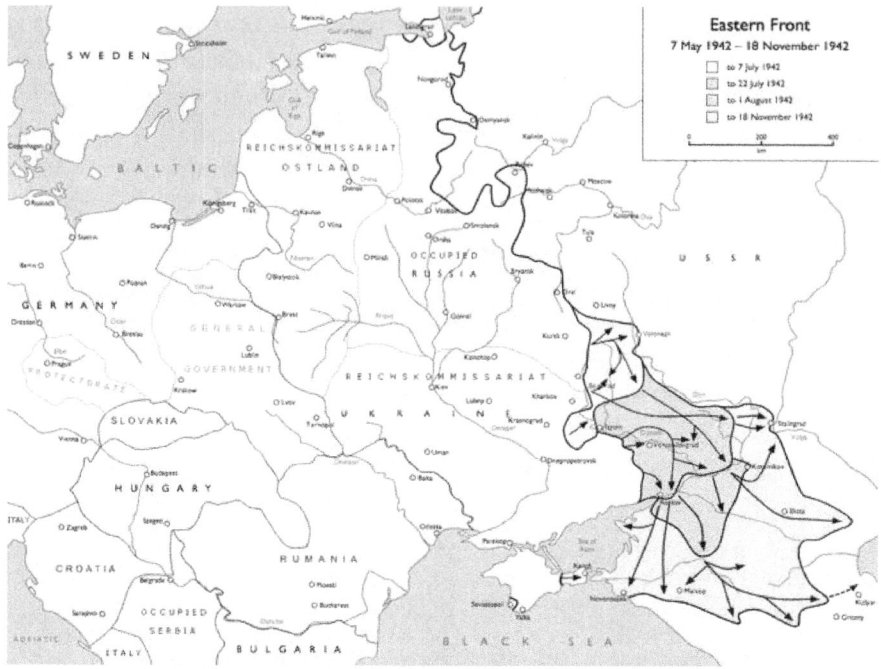

Operation Blau, or Blue, was a massive operation that lasted months and stretched hundreds of miles deep into southern Russia.[2]

Operation Blue was a massive strategic offensive involving over one and a half million soldiers in Army Group South. The men moved east and southeast toward the Volga and the Caucasus Mountains. Army Group South was subdivided into two parts. Army Group A, comprising the German 1st Panzer Army, 11th and 17th Armies, and the 3rd Romanian Army, would drive for the Caucasus as part of Operation Edelweiss. Army Group B (4th Panzer Army, 2nd and 6th Armies, the Hungarian 2nd Army, the Romanian 4th Army, and the Italian 8th Army) would head east.

General Erich von Manstein's 11th Army had been laying siege to the Black Sea port of Sevastopol since October 1941. On July 4th, 1942, the city fell. The 11th Army was then able to push across the Crimea and east across the Kerch Straits, between the Sea of Azov and the Black Sea, and into the western end of the Caucasus Mountain range. General Friedrich von Paulus's 6th Army, fresh from the massive defeat they had inflicted on Timoshenko's forces, drove east toward the Volga River and the city of Stalingrad.

Once again, the panzer divisions were in the front of the battle. They were the "tip of the spear" and advanced rapidly across the flat open steppe to the Volga River.

"The Germans had gone all the way from the Don to the Volga in a single day, and it seemed a great achievement. They had now reached what they considered to be the border of Asia as well as Hitler's ultimate objective, the Archangelsk-Astrakhan line. Many felt that the war was as good as over. They took triumphant photographs of each other posing on their tanks, and also snaps of the smoke clouds rising from Stalingrad. A Luftwaffe fighter ace and his wingman, spotting the panzers below, performed victory rolls."[i]

However, as the Germans got farther east and farther south, they began to experience the same problems they had encountered during Operation Barbarossa the year before. Supplies, spare parts, and replacements could not keep up with the speed of the advance. Combat casualties and wear and tear greatly reduced the strength of the divisions. Soviet resistance was stiffening, and new Russian divisions were pushed into the battle. As the 6th Army moved into the major urban and industrial sprawl of Stalingrad, the advance slowed considerably. Although as much as 90 percent of the city had fallen into German hands, the street fighting was bloody, and advancement was slow. Stalin was more than willing to feed more soldiers into this fight, and the key advantage of the panzers—their mobility—was reduced to nothing amidst the rubble of Stalingrad. Soviet soldiers hid in the ruined buildings armed with cheap anti-tank rifles and "Molotov cocktail" petrol bombs.

Meanwhile, farther south, the 1st Panzer Army made it to the Caucasus Mountains. German mountain troops even managed to plant swastika flags atop Mount Elbrus, the highest mountain peak in Europe.[ii] However, resistance remained fierce, and many of the oilfields were sufficiently destroyed or damaged enough to require extensive years-long repairs. The German panzer and aircraft continued to suffer from fuel shortages and were in a very precarious situation. They were at the very limit of their supply lines.

---

[i] Beevor, A., *The Second World War*, (Weidenfeld and Nicolson: London, 2012), pp.337-338.

[ii] The flags were removed by Soviet mountaineers the following February.

Operation Blue seemed to have gained a lot of ground for Hitler's Wehrmacht. On the maps, it certainly looked impressive. But it had come at a great cost in terms of time, money, casualties, and equipment. There was little of tangible and strategic value to show for it. Stalingrad continued to be a contest of wills between the two dictators, with neither willing to give way. As winter came, the German 6th Army, along with its Romanian, Hungarian, and Italian allies, hunkered down in and around the ruins of Stalingrad. The Axis offensive power had been exhausted. They could only hope that the Soviets were feeling the same way.

Marshal Georgy Zhukov was one of Stalin's most trusted commanders after his defensive successes at Leningrad and the critical counterattack at Moscow that had saved the city. He was charged with putting together another powerful counter punch, this time to the north and south of Stalingrad. He would use the winter weather as cover for large-scale military movements. The Soviets had discovered that while the Germans held the bulk of Stalingrad, the flanks of the city were manned by weaker and less combat-capable Hungarians, Romanians, and Italians. It was here that the Soviets would strike with power and surprise on November 19th, 1942. Germany's allies quickly crumbled, and Stalingrad, which had around 300,000, was surrounded. The famous Stuka pilot, Hans-Ulrich Rudel, was scathing in his criticism of the collapse of the German allies:

"On the return flight we again observe the fleeing Rumanians; it is a good thing for them I have run out of ammunition to stop this cowardly rout. They have abandoned everything; their easily defended positions, their heavy artillery, their ammunition dumps. Their cowardice is certain to cause a debacle along the whole front. Unopposed, the Soviet advance rolls forward to Kalatsch. And with Kalatsch in their hands they now close a semi-circle round our half of Stalingrad."[i]

On November 23rd, the trap closed around Stalingrad. Although shocked, the German high command, as well as the soldiers in the city, were initially confident that this was a temporary setback. General von Paulus, the commander of the German 6th Army, was forbidden to attempt a breakout. The Luftwaffe was committed by its chief, Hermann Göring, to resupply the beleaguered city from the air. Despite Göring's bravado-filled pronouncements, the daily food and fuel requirements for

---

[i] Rudel, H., *Stuka Pilot*, (Ballantine Books: New York, 1958), p.84.

a force of several hundred thousand men were entirely beyond the Luftwaffe pilots, despite many brave efforts by the pilots. Many aircraft were shot down as they tried to fly into and out of the city. A trail of blackened, wrecked Ju-52 tri-motor transport aircraft lined the snow-bound approach routes to the city. They were shot down by concentrated batteries of Soviet anti-aircraft guns. Horses were shot and eaten, and the 6th Army slowly began to starve. Their predicament was made infinitely worse by the bitter winter weather conditions.

Von Manstein, who was now experienced in mobile armored warfare, was charged with punching through the Soviet lines to relieve the city. After some early progress, Operation Wintergewitter ("Winter Storm") came to no avail. The men were bogged down due to poor weather and stiff Soviet resistance. By the end of January 1943, General von Paulus had surrendered. Almost 100,000 soldiers of a once proud and powerful force of over half a million men were marched east to prison camps or suffered a frozen death en route. Germany had suffered its most resounding defeat of the Second World War thus far. The loss of Stalingrad and the 6th Army is generally seen by military historians as the crucial turning point of the war in the east.

"Hitler heard the news of the surrender in silence. He apparently stared into his vegetable soup. But the next day his anger exploded against Paulus for having failed to shoot himself ... In Moscow, the bells of the Kremlin rang out a victory peal ... In Germany, radio stations were ordered to play solemn music ...Word spread rapidly in Germany, mainly from those listening in secret to the BBC, that Moscow had announced the capture of 91,000. The shock of the defeat was overwhelming in Germany. Only Nazi fanatics still thoughts the war could be won."[i]

---

[i] Beevor, A., *The Second World War*, (Weidenfeld and Nicolson: London, 2012), pp.399-400.

Chapter 3 – Spring 1943: Kharkov and the Planning for Kursk

"Seldom has a major offensive been as obvious to the enemy as the Germans' Operation Citadel to cut off the Soviet salient round Kursk."[i]

The loss of Stalingrad blew a massive hole in the German front line. Powerful Soviet counterattacks from November 1942 to February 1943 effectively reversed all the gains made by Operation Blue the previous summer.[3]

---

[i] Beevor, A., *The Second World War*, (Weidenfeld and Nicolson: London, 2012), p.469.

Collapse and Counterattack

The loss of the 6th Army left a massive gap in the German front line. The Soviet forces took full advantage of this and surged forward on a broad front of hundreds of miles, stretching in a line from Orel in central Russia to Stalingrad and down south almost to Grozny. From a German perspective, the threat to the four armies in Army Group A in the Caucasus was the most urgent. As Soviet tank units pushed aggressively westward from Stalingrad to Rostov, on the coast of the Sea of Azov, they threatened another mass encirclement, one even greater than that of Stalingrad. The Soviets were to be thwarted in this larger ambition because the highly mobile and flexible use of German panzer and motorized divisions under von Manstein slowed the Soviet advance.

Von Manstein had to battle with Adolf Hitler's stubborn resistance to accept retreats of any sort. The Soviets moved relentlessly forward. Voronezh was recaptured on January 25th, 1943, and Rostov, the "Gate to the Caucasus," was retaken on February 14th. The German armies in the Caucasus managed to retreat through Rostov before it was captured or moved west to hold a small bridgehead at Kuban in the west Caucasus, just opposite the Crimea.

Of greater significance for what was to come, the key railway junction of Kursk was recaptured by the Soviets on February 8th, and four Soviet tank corps pressed ahead toward Kharkov. For the third (and not the last) time, Kharkov would subjected to a major battle. Von Manstein employed his still-potent panzer divisions very effectively. His force was augmented by the very well-equipped and motivated 2nd SS Panzer Corps. Rather than fighting a painful and protracted battle for the city of Kharkov itself, which Hitler had demanded, von Manstein pulled back and allowed the Soviets to enter the city. Von Manstein's fluid and flexible set of armored counter punches enveloped the Soviet units from the flanks, destroying most of the force and causing the remnants to flee in disarray. From mid-February to mid-March, the outnumbered German panzer units fought the Soviets to a standstill and recaptured Kharkov.

It was an impressive display of generalship by von Manstein—and at just the time when it was needed. The Soviet advance had been rebuffed, and the front lines began to stabilize. It was March by that point. The thaw of winter was in full effect, bringing thick mud to the battlefields, the supply lines, and the rear areas of both sides. The Germans and Soviets had battered each other to a standstill.

What Was Next for Germany on the Eastern Front?

At this point in the spring, the German and Soviet armies seized the opportunity and began the urgent process of regrouping, rearming, and reequipping for the inevitable summer campaigning season. The last few months had confirmed that the Soviet forces were no longer poorly trained and equipped. The Soviets had benefited from the painful lessons dealt to them by the Germans. They were adapting impressively. With most of the Russian armament factories now safely relocated behind the Ural Mountains, beyond bombing reach of the Luftwaffe, thousands of tanks, self-propelled guns, aircraft, and artillery pieces were being mass produced. In the hands of skilled and ruthless senior commanders such as Zhukov, Soviet forces were now capable of taking the fight to the Germans with large-scale and complex operations. The summer of 1943 was going to be very different from the previous summer.

The Soviets were emboldened and confident. More crucially, they were able to quickly replace any losses on the battlefield. The Germans were pushed onto the back foot after six months of defeats. However, they were still very powerful, with highly experienced military commanders operating effective, proven equipment. And new equipment was about to come.

The German high command debated what to do. The German Army no longer looked as if it had the capability to launch a massive strategic summer offensive along the lines of Operation Blue and certainly not on the scale of Operation Barbarossa. But to cede the initiative—to sit back and let the Soviet army come at them at a time and place of its choosing—also seemed unthinkable. It would have been a clear admission of failure in the east. Hitler agonized and dithered.

The Bigger Picture

While both armies regroup and the Russian mud slowly dries, it is a good time to take a look at the bigger picture and what was going on in the rest of the world. What impact did global developments have on the decisions regarding the Eastern Front in the summer of 1943?

On almost every front, the tide of war was turning against the Nazis. The second half of 1942 had brought little but bad news for the Germans and their allies.

The Battle for the Atlantic, Germany's submarine war to starve Britain by preventing food, troops, and fuel from crossing the ocean, had turned in the Allies' favor. Developments in radar technology caused German "U-boats" to be sunk faster than they could interfere with Allied convoys.

With the arrival of US strategic bombing airpower in the United Kingdom in late 1942, the Allies were able to seriously increase their bombing campaign against Germany. With the British bombing during the night and Americans bombing during the day, German industrial regions—the ones that were producing the tanks, guns, and aircraft that Germany desperately needed on the Eastern Front—were subject to continuous and highly destructive bombardments. On May 17th, 1943, British Lancaster bombers conducted an audacious raid against dams providing water for the Ruhr industrial effort, which greatly hampered German effort for weeks afterward. This one mission struck physical and psychological blows against the German home front.

On May 30th, 1942, the first "Thousand Bomber Raid" hit Cologne. By August 1943, American B-17 bombers were in range of the Ploesti oilfields in Romania that the German war industry depended on. Increasing numbers of German aircraft, anti-aircraft guns, and manpower had to be retained in Germany to protect the factories and cities; not even Berlin was immune to air raids.

Three other "turning points" should be mentioned on top of the crushing defeat at Stalingrad. In the war in the Pacific between America and Japan, Germany's ally, the Japanese fleet suffered a serious reversal at the Battle of Midway in June 1942.

In North Africa, another advocate of blitzkrieg warfare, General Erwin Rommel, had met failure. The back-and-forth contest along the Mediterranean coast had seen Rommel's Afrika Korps, operating a shoestring mechanized force of two understrength panzer divisions, advance to El Alamein, rolling back Allied forces and putting Egypt and the Suez Canal in real jeopardy. However, the Afrika Korps ground to a halt there. Its men were beset by the same problems experienced by Army Group South in Russia: extended supply lines, lack of spares, and lack of replacements. The First Battle of El Alamein, which took place in July 1942, saw Rommel's attack stopped dead.

The Second Battle of El Alamein in October 1942 was a triumph of military logistical buildup. The British, under General Bernard Montgomery, had shortened supply lines and were able to amass artillery, fuel, trucks, and hundreds of tanks, including the new American medium tank, the Sherman. Rommel, on the other hand, was right at the outer limit of his supply chain and lost many of his supply ships in the Mediterranean to Allied submarines. He struggled to provide for his German-Italian army. The British 8th Army had twice as many soldiers and twice as many tanks when the offensive advanced and broke through the Afrika Korps positions. Rommel's forces were down to their last days of fuel and their last few tanks as they retreated back across Egypt and Libya and into Tunisia.

And the problems did not stop there. While Rommel was assailed by the 8th Army to the east (and thrown a thousand miles backward), the Americans landed in Morocco in November to the west to engage in Operation Torch. The Afrika Korps was trapped. Rommel retreated into Tunisia. Hemmed in on all sides, he put up a valiant defense. His resources were still limited, but he was given one precious battalion of the new Tiger tanks that were slowly coming off the production lines.

Rommel defeated the Americans at the Battle of Kasserine Pass, but it was to no avail: the Americans learned quickly, and the British were already highly advanced in their application of air and ground cooperation. On May 13th, 1943, German forces in Tunisia surrendered. Although some experienced units were evacuated, the defeat was ultimately comparable to the losses at Stalingrad—over a quarter of a million German and Italian soldiers entered captivity in what the jubilant Allied media took pleasure in dubbing "Tunisgrad." With Tunisia captured, the German and Italian presence in North Africa came to an end.

The logical next step for the Allies would be an invasion of Sicily and Italy. It was surely just a matter of time. From a German perspective, mainland Europe was at an imminent threat. The decision for the Allies to invade Sicily emerged from the January 1943 Casablanca conference. Operation Husky, the Allied plan for the invasion, was finalized on April 27th, 1943, with the actual invasion to take place in early July. As history now shows, the events in the Mediterranean that summer were to have a profound effect on the Eastern Front.

Hitler's Dilemma

This was the military situation in which Hitler and his generals found themselves. There was recognition that some sort of strategic action was probably needed on the Eastern Front if only to demonstrate that German military capability was not exhausted. Hitler's allies—the Finns,

Romanians, Hungarians, Italians, Spanish, and Slovaks—had already suffered mightily on the Eastern Front and elsewhere. Without a powerful blow in the east, Hitler was worried that his allies might start to conclude that the Nazis were no longer all-powerful and start striking peace deals of their own.

But What to Do in the East?

Even Hitler appeared to finally understand that a massive offensive on the scale of Operation Blue (Barbarossa was long since dismissed as any kind of option) was probably beyond the reach of his forces. Hitler cast around for options. After Stalingrad, he no longer appeared fully confident in his instincts. He got distracted by ideas of attacking Sweden. He considered an attempt to capture the besieged city of Leningrad. Two very small-scale operations in the Kharkov region, Habicht and Panther, were developed. They would have tidied up the front lines east of Kharkov and pushed the Soviet forces back a little.

These ideas were ultimately dismissed. His generals were uneasy. Some felt that an attack of any kind on the Eastern Front in 1943 was unnecessary. However, speaking their mind directly to the Führer was a high-risk business, so most trod carefully and kept their thoughts to themselves.

Forehand or Backhand?

In the spring of 1943, both the Russians and the Germans were looking at summer offensives in some capacity. Both were uncertain whether it was better to get the first blow in or to wait and absorb the enemy's attack before launching a powerful counterattack once the enemy was exhausted. Erich von Manstein described the dilemma from the German side with the use of tennis metaphors in his post-war memoirs:

"What [Hitler] ultimately had to decide was whether the overall situation allowed us to wait for the Russians to start an offensive and then to hit them hard 'on the backhand' at the first good opportunity, or whether we should attack as early as possible ourselves and—still within the framework of a strategic defensive—strike a limited blow 'on the forehand'"[i]

---

[i] Manstein, E. von, *Lost Victories*, (Zenith Press: Minneapolis, 2004), pp445-446.

At this stage of the war, Stalin appears to have been more willing to listen to his generals and take their advice. He had made several poor judgments that had cost the Red Army heavily. The Soviet leadership went through the same analytical process: was it better to attack first or second? They came up with a different answer to the Germans.

"On 8 April Zhukov responded, predicting that the Germans would first attack Kursk, then attempt to encircle Soviet troops south of the bulge, and finally turn against Moscow ... 'I do not consider it necessary for our troops to mount a preventive offensive in the next few days. It will be better if we wear the enemy out in defensive action, destroy his tanks, and then, taking in fresh reserves, by going over to an all-out offensive, we will finish off the enemy's main grouping.'"[i]

Most of the other senior generals agreed, and Stalin became persuaded that this was the better course of action. In April, the Soviet forces identified where the attack was most likely to come and began to prepare to meet the attack, constructing extensive defensive positions in and around Kursk.

On March 13th, 1943, the German high command issued Operational Order Number Five. It was a general instruction telling the army in Russia to refit and prepare for operations. A potential German attack in the Kharkov region was mentioned, although no specifics were given at this stage. All units were to provide weekly updates on troop and equipment numbers so the high command could get a good sense of which formations could be considered combat ready. For this campaigning season, the German planners had to contend with the extreme likelihood of major Soviet offensives, perhaps even simultaneously, and it was not clear where they might come from and when.

After the chaotic conflicts in the early spring, the Germans had emerged relatively successful. Kharkov became a relatively firm base for the German forces. Orel, two hundred miles due north, was also secure. However, Kursk, a road and rail hub between these two cities, was in Russian hands. The Kursk salient now jutted one hundred miles westward into the German lines. It was an obvious target for a military pincer movement.

---

[i] Glantz, D., and House, J., *The Battle of Kursk*, (University Press of Kansas: Kansas, 1999), p.29.

Spring/summer of 1943. This was the situation immediately after the recapture of Kharkov.⁴

The concept for the Kursk operation came from General Kurt Zeitzler, the German chief of the Army General Staff. From even the most casual glance at a map of the situation in the spring of 1943, one could see the most effective way to deal with the Kursk salient was to mount simultaneous attacks from the north and south at the shoulders of the bulge to meet somewhere in the middle, if possible at Kursk itself. Kursk was a key transport hub for road and rail networks in the area. If implemented successfully and, above all, *quickly*, the Soviet forces would be trapped and forced to surrender. Perhaps the Germans would even open a large hole in the Soviet lines, which could offer opportunities for exploitation for the panzer divisions. At the very least, the front line would be shortened, which would allow some German divisions to be released, either to go into the reserve or be redeployed for other operations.

Heinz Guderian, the highly experienced blitzkrieg veteran, was now inspector general of armored troops, which meant he was in charge of tank production and developing new tank types. He was working energetically—with some success—to ensure that all the panzer divisions were brought up to something approaching full strength. His ambition that every panzer division should have four hundred tanks was no longer possible. German tank production was harried day and night by British and American strategic bombers, and Germany was not capable of reaching the necessary production levels. Even to have two hundred tanks under command was extremely rare for a panzer division on the Eastern Front. The latest redesign of the panzer division structure, which was effectively a downsizing, required that a full-strength panzer division should have 160 tanks. In reality, except for perhaps at the very start of an offensive, it was common for tank units to have half or even a quarter of their full authorized strength after a few days or weeks of intense action.

Guderian disagreed with Hitler and the generals. He was of the strong opinion that no significant offensive operations should take place on the Eastern Front in 1943 at all and that resources should be conserved and gathered until decisive operations could be undertaken in 1944. He was also one of the few generals willing to go toe to toe with Hitler in a disagreement (he had already been sacked once because of this).

This remarkable and highly revealing exchange reportedly took place between Hitler and Guderian on May 10th, when the Kursk objective had already been decided upon.

Guderian stated, "It's a matter of profound indifference to the world whether we hold Kursk or not. I repeat my question: Why do we want to attack in the East at all this year?"

Hitler replied, "You're quite right. Whenever I think of this attack my stomach turns over."[i]

An attack on Kursk was quite an obvious idea. It was unlikely to allow for any form of surprise or initiative to be gained. Stalin and his generals quickly understood the risks to the Kursk salient and actively implemented defensive measures. On April 8th, Marshal Georgy Zhukov provided the following assessment to Stalin regarding likely German activities in the summer.

"Having suffered serious losses in the winter campaign of 1942/43, the enemy would not appear to be able to build up big reserves by the spring to resume the offensive on the Caucasus and to push forward to the Volga ... Owing to the inadequacy of large reserves, in the spring and

---

[i] Glantz, D., and House, J., *The Battle of Kursk*, (University Press of Kansas: Kansas, 1999), p.3.

first half of the summer of 1943 the enemy will be forced to launch offensive operations on a smaller front ... there are groupings deployed against our Central, Voronezh and South-Western Fronts, I believe the enemy's main offensive will be spearheaded at these fronts, in order to rout our forces on this sector ... the enemy will evidently deal the blow with his Orel-Kromy grouping in the enveloping movement around Kursk from the north-east and likewise with the Belgorod-Kharkov grouping from the south-east."[i]

On April 15th, Operational Order Number Six was issued. It was very specific about the task ahead, instructing German forces to be ready to conduct operations against the Kursk salient at any time after April 28th and with six days' notice, assuming the weather was favorable.

However, it seemed that Hitler was never fully committed to the Kursk attack, which had now acquired the title of Operation Citadel ("Zitadelle" in German). The date of the offensive would change several times. It was postponed until July, as Hitler obsessed over tank production lines, worried that he did not yet have enough armored forces and new tanks to guarantee a successful operation.

---

[i] Zhukov, G., *Reminiscences and Reflections*, Volume II, (Progress Publishers: Moscow, 1985), pp.150-152.

Chapter 4 – The Battlefield and the Opponents

Climate and Terrain

The summer season in the area around Kursk has a climate best described as warm summer continental. There are occasional heatwaves but also frequent periods of overcast, cloudy weather and periodic showers, with rainfall of some sort on average eight or nine days a month in June, July, and August. July is the warmest month, with an average high of 25 degrees Celsius (77 degrees Fahrenheit) and a low of 15 degrees (59 degrees Fahrenheit).

The terrain that was fought over was part of the Central Russian Upland that forms a watershed of rivers that drain south into the Black Sea and southeast into the Caspian Sea. The area is predominantly agricultural—rolling farming countryside on a large plateau, scattered with many small hamlets and villages in between low hills. The fertile soil is black, but the shallow topsoil is a yellowish gray. This means that when trenches and other fortifications are being dug, the black soil is quickly reached, and this is easy to spot from the air. One striking feature that is very evident from a look at Google Earth is the number of gullies and ravines.[i] These water features greatly interfered with movement. They

---

[i] See Google Earth coordinates: 50.956261034962l7, 36.711501885875888. This location is about four miles south of Prokhorovka. The ravines are clearly visible, and their defensive potential would have been significant. A scroll around the area reveals many, many more such

made excellent anti-tank ditches and often provided good defensive positions, cover, and concealment. As the farmers plowed around them, it allowed trees, bushes, and other vegetation to line the edges of the ravines, blocking ground-level visibility across them. The ravines were often passable to vehicles, particularly tracked vehicles. However, after a sudden downpour, the steep sides would quickly become muddy, making them suddenly impassable.

The Soviet Army at Kursk—The Soldier

The Soviet army had come a long way since its near collapse in the summer of 1941. It was now a fearsome opponent for the Germans.[i]

The Soviets still relied more on massed forces rather than tactical finesse. "Human wave" attacks, with row upon row of soldiers surging forward in a mass, were a feature—and a great fear of the Germans—of warfare on the Eastern Front. The tactic was reminiscent of the Napoleonic era. Although painfully wasteful in lives, it could be a traumatic experience for the enemy.

"But we were watching the veteran: his eyes were growing wider and wider, and so was his mouth, which seemed ready to howl. The stabs had shut up too; we all followed the direction of our gunner's eyes. In the remote distance, a thin black line stretched from one end of the horizon to the other, and was moving towards us like a wave rolling toward the shore. We stood watching for the moment: the line was dense, and somehow unreal. Then the veteran shouted in a voice which paralysed us with fear: 'It's the Siberians! They're here! There must be at least a million of them!' ... In the distance, a confused tumult of thousands of roaring voices swelled like a hurricane wind."[ii]

The Soviet command structure was still weak. It was still a struggle to maintain flexible command and control of its units when in action. Every German tank was fitted with a radio, but radios were not a common feature in Soviet tanks at the start of the war. Flags were used to direct tank formations during a battle. And the communist regime did not incentivize independent thinking. Officer initiative was poor; commanders were very fearful of going beyond their orders for fear of

---

gullies.

[i] Glantz, D., and House, J., *The Battle of Kursk*, (University Press of Kansas: Kansas, 1999), p.33.

[ii] Sajer, G., *The Forgotten Soldier*, (Sphere Books Ltd: London, 1980), pp.243-244.

punishment and even death. Officers would rather send their request for instructions up the chain of command, with a delay at every level, rather than decide for themselves instantly on the spot. During the 1930s, a paranoid Joseph Stalin had killed many of his best commanders in a purge that had stifled the development of the officer corps for a generation. On the battlefield, smaller but more mobile German units frequently outfought their larger Soviet counterparts because they were able to decide and react far more quickly.

However, the individual Soviet soldier was tough and resilient. He was capable of undergoing hardships that many other European armies would not survive.

"The German commanders who prepared for Kursk thought of their opponents as 'tenacious but inept' fighters who had difficulty coordinating the many ingredients necessary for modern warfare."[i]

Both soldiers and commanders alike appeared indifferent to the number of casualties they suffered. Infantry divisions and tank corps alike could be flung into battle heedless of losses and compelled to keep attacking until they were almost wiped out. Only then were they withdrawn and replenished. The soldiers could exist on minimal supplies and in extreme temperatures, including the brutal Russian winter. They would willingly sacrifice themselves in defense of a building, bunker, or strongpoint when the realities of the situation demanded surrender or retreat. Conversely, if caught by surprise in the flank or rear, the Russian troops could suddenly collapse and be routed. General Friedrich von Mellenthin, who would become chief of staff of the 48th Panzer Corps during the Battle of Kursk, devoted a chapter of his memoirs to describing the nature of the Russian soldier.

"The Russian is quite unpredictable; today he does not care whether his flanks are threatened or not, tomorrow he trembles at the idea of having his flanks exposed. He disregards accepted tactical principles but sticks to the letter of his field manuals ... The Russian soldier is independent of seasons or environment; he is a good soldier everywhere and under any conditions ... In an incredibly short time he literally disappears into the ground, digging himself in and making instinctive use of the terrain ... The Russian soldier properly dug in, hugging Mother

---

[i] Glantz, D., and House, J., *The Battle of Kursk*, (University Press of Kansas: Kansas, 1999), p.33.

Earth, and well camouflaged, is an enemy doubly dangerous."[i]

General Dwight D. Eisenhower would later describe in his 1948 book, *Crusade in Europe*, a revealing conversation he had had with Marshal Georgy Zhukov.

"Marshal Zhukov gave me a matter-of-fact statement of his practice, which was, roughly, 'There are two kinds of mines; one is the personnel mine and the other is the vehicular mine. When we come to a mine field our infantry attacks exactly as if it were not there. The losses we get from personnel mines we consider only equal to those we would have gotten from machine guns and artillery if the Germans had chosen to defend that particular area with strong bodies of troops instead of with mine fields.'"[ii]

During Barbarossa, Soviet units that particularly distinguished themselves in battle could be given the honorific title of "Guards," which would be added to the unit title between the number of the formation and the type of unit, such as tank, infantry, or airborne. Guards units were considered elite formations and were expected to perform better than regular units. Several Guards units were to fight at Kursk, including General Pavel Rotmistrov's 5th Guards Tank Army, which we will meet during the Battle of Prokhorovka, located southeast of Kursk. The army was raised in February 1943 by combining three Guards tank units—the 3rd Guards Tank Corps, the 29th Guards Tank Corps, and the 5th Guards Mechanised Corps.

The Soviet Army at Kursk—The Equipment

The existence of the T-34, the KV-1, and the KV-2, all powerful tanks, had come as a serious shock to the German Army in the early days of Operation Barbarossa. The T-34 remained at the core of the Soviet tank forces at Kursk. Other self-propelled guns had also been introduced; they were essentially turretless tracked armored vehicles with thick, sloped armor. These were designed to mount powerful guns: 85 mm, 122 mm, and even 152 mm pieces. These were highly credible pieces of combat equipment. Russian armored vehicles were robust, uncomplicated, and reliable in all weather extremes. But perhaps the most decisive strength of the tank forces lay in the sheer numbers that

---

[i] Mellenthin, F. von, *Panzer Battles*, (Futura Publications Ltd: London, 1979), pp.350-352.

[ii] Eisenhower, D., *Crusade in Europe*, (William Heinemann Limited: London, 1949), pp.510-511.

could be driven off the production lines.

"It is estimated that 1,800 T-34's were produced in 1940, 2,800 in 1941, and over 30,000 T-34's were produced between 1942-44. Manufacturing efficiencies enabled these production increases. Between 1941 and 1943, both the cost and time it took to create a T-34 were cut in half."[i]

Let's compare this to the production of the German Panzer VI, the legendary Tiger tank. Less than 1,500 Tigers were ever built during the entire Second World War. These had to be divided between service in Russia, Tunisia, and Italy, as well as in what would become the intensely fought Western Front, from France to Germany.[ii] No panzer division was ever fully equipped with the Tiger tank. There were never enough to go around.

Soviet infantry weapons were also robust, solid, dependable, and easy to use. The Maxim heavy machine gun, designed before the First World War, was used in the Russo-Ukraine conflict in the 2020s. Handheld submachine guns were simple and easy to mass produce. The PPSh-41 was simply made; it was stamped from sheet metal for ease of productivity and was available in the millions. The Soviets amassed a powerful arsenal of anti-tank guns, artillery pieces, and mortars of all calibers and made extensive use of large-scale artillery barrages in offense and defense. However, infantry anti-tank capability was weaker. By 1943, handheld rocket launchers were being employed by the Americans (in the form of the bazooka) and the Germans (the Panzerfaust). The Soviet infantry had an obsolete 14.5 mm (0.5 inch) anti-tank rifle and was also routinely expected to tackle enemy tanks with mines, grenades, and improvised Molotov cocktails (petrol bombs).

One final word should be said about a major group of fighters that had an impact on the Battle of Kursk but was not present on the battlefield. Thousands of Russian partisans operated in the rear areas behind the German lines. Some of these were local members of the population—farmers whose villages had been overrun, their homes and agricultural produce looted by the Germans. Many others were Soviet

---

[i] 'T-34 Tank,' *Russia in global perspective*, Website accessed 12 June 2024, https://russiaglobal.omeka.fas.harvard.edu/exhibits/show/objects/politics/t34#_edn7

[ii] 'Building the Tiger Tank,' The Tank Museum, 16 Mar. 2020, https://tankmuseum.org/article/building-a-tiger-tank/

soldiers who had been overrun and bypassed by the Germans during the large-scale operations of Barbarossa in 1941. By the spring of 1943, the partisans were well organized, well supplied by parachute drops, and well coordinated by the Soviet high command. Partisans conducted thousands of small-scale raids before, during, and after the German offensive at Kursk, ambushing already tenuous German supply lines. They blew up railway lines and destroyed locomotive engines and wagons. The partisan war was brutal, with atrocities committed on both sides. Partisans captured by the Germans were routinely shot or hung. However, the partisans were instrumental in hampering every aspect of the German offensive.[i]

The German Army at Kursk—The Soldier

When the German soldiers entered Russia, they were extremely confident to the point of arrogance. The German Army had done the unimaginable. It had defeated the best modern armies that Europe could line up against it. The German emphasis was on rapid activity, quick decisions, and the acceptance of responsibility and initiative right down to the lowest level of fighting men. The combination of all arms—air, artillery, tanks, engineers, and infantry—into flexible and adaptive teams was a crucial part of the German military's ethos. Some historians simply call this "blitzkrieg." This was a term, perhaps surprisingly, that the German Army did not recognize. The Germans preferred the expression "Auftragstaktik," which essentially meant outlining the task to the soldier in general terms and allowing the soldier to decide how best to achieve that goal without detailed orders or excessive involvement of higher command structures. Auftragstaktik relied on individual initiative, flexibility, and trust. It was why heavily outnumbered German forces outfought Soviet troops repeatedly throughout the war on the Eastern Front.[ii]

A particular German skill was the ability to improvise combat units from remnants of other forces in an emergency, such as a sudden Soviet breakthrough. These makeshift forces often fought with real effectiveness and were known as Kampfgruppe, or battle groups. Critics

---

[i] Caidin, M., *The Tigers Are Burning*, (Pinnacle Books, Los Angeles, 1980), pp.143-145

[ii] Vandergriff, D., 'How the Germans Defined Auftragstaktik: What Mission Command is - and –is not,' Small Wars Journal, 21 June 2018, https://smallwarsjournal.com/jrnl/art/how-germans-defined-auftragstaktik-what-mission-command-and-not

of the Kampfgruppe practice note that this "cannibalization" of units simply reflected the collapse of German combat resources in Russia and elsewhere in the later stages of the war. By this time, there were neither the reinforcements nor the infrastructure to be able to withdraw units for rest and replace them with other complete units.

The Germans had several elite formations fighting at Kursk, the most controversial of which was the Waffen-SS divisions. They were very effective combat troops. The SS were fiercely loyal to Hitler and committed many atrocities against enemy soldiers and civilians wherever they fought. However, the Eastern Front saw the most brutal actions of SS units. The Nazi regime had inculcated into the SS the belief the Slavic peoples were subhuman, fit only to work as slaves for the Nazis.

Even the regular German Army viewed the SS with suspicion and distaste. One of the SS divisions at Kursk, the 3rd Totenkopf ("Death's Head") Panzergrenadier Division, was originally formed from German concentration camp guards. By this stage of the war, the three SS divisions in the 2nd SS Panzer Corps had all committed atrocities, including in the Polish campaign. They would go on to commit more war crimes during the rest of the war.

From the 1930s onward, the SS had exacting standards for recruitment in terms of physical fitness and ethnic origin. The SS had the pick of the best recruits and routinely received the best training and equipment. SS divisions were generally bigger organizations than their regular army counterparts. During the course of the war, the SS expanded in numbers, and the quality of the recruits declined. They were generally at the forefront of key military attacks or would be the basis of a reserve to restore the front line if the enemy broke through. They were feared by all and gained a reputation for their ruthless effectiveness.

At Kursk, three SS mechanized "panzergrenadier" divisions were grouped into the 2nd SS Panzer Corps. They were under SS General Paul Hausser and were structured and equipped essentially as panzer divisions with above-average strength. They would be at the center of some of the most intense battles at Kursk.

One other elite formation should also be mentioned since it was in the middle of the fiercest fighting. The Grossdeutschland ("Greater Germany") division was not an SS unit, but it was treated like one in terms of receiving the best recruits and equipment. It had originally been raised as a ceremonial guard unit in the 1920s, but it had expanded into an infantry regiment by the outbreak of the war in 1939. Because of its good performance on the Eastern Front, it was increased in size in 1942, going from a regiment (about two thousand men) to a panzergrenadier division (about fourteen thousand men) by May 1943, in time for the Kursk offensive. Significantly, it was accorded the honor of receiving the first brand-new Panzer Mark V "Panther" tanks. Two hundred of them were attached as a new tank brigade to the division just in time for the battle.

The German Army at Kursk—The Equipment

Throughout the Second World War, Germany was famous for producing inventive, high-quality, and militarily effective combat equipment for the air, sea, and land. Many are still famous and recognized as icons of the time—the MG-42 machine gun, the 88 mm anti-aircraft/anti-tank gun, the Messerschmitt Me-109, the Ju 87 Stuka dive bomber, the Me-262 jet fighter, and the Panther and Tiger tanks. The innovative late-war assault rifle, the Sturmgewehr-44, was very similar to the Soviet post-war AK-47 and likely influenced its design.

However, there were major and interwoven problems with German equipment generally during the war. German manufacturers competed for funding, resources, and Hitler's attention. Hitler himself could easily get sidetracked by expensive and entirely battlefield-inappropriate vanity projects, such as the Maus super heavy tank, which, at around 170 tons (the Tiger tank, itself considered rather a heavy beast, was 56 tons), would never be capable of crossing rural bridges. The Maus project saw three German companies compete with each other and consumed money and manpower from 1943 to 1945. It never saw active service.

Even battlefield equipment was made in an unnecessarily complex way, and manufacturing processes could vary from factory to factory. Little regard was paid to the standardization of weapon systems and ensuring components and spare parts could fit a variety of vehicles or machinery. As a result, key German weapons were not best suited to mass production. Where the Germans could produce hundreds of a given weapon, the Soviets and the Americans could produce thousands. In a purely numbers game, the German Army could never win.

The three significant tank systems that saw service at Kursk—the Tiger, Panther, and Elefant (technically not a tank but a self-propelled gun)—were all victims of these inherent inefficiencies and flaws in the Nazi design, development, and production process. As a result, they were all much less effective than they could have been.

The Numbers and Structure of the Opposing Forces

The numbers of troops, tanks, guns, and aircraft involved in the Battle of Kursk were colossal, although precise data is hard to pin down, and a variety of sources say different things. Not all the armies, corps, and divisions in and around the Kursk salient were directly involved in fighting during the crucial first half of July 1943. Nevertheless, troop numbers were in the millions, and the tanks, aircraft, and guns were in the thousands and even tens of thousands. The Germans had three-quarters of a million soldiers for the operation in the region. They were supported by three thousand tanks and assault guns. The Soviets had one and a half million soldiers and approximately five thousand tanks and assault guns.[1] However, these forces were not all in action at the same time, and in key parts of the battlefield, much smaller numbers were involved.

The basic combat "building block" of both armies on the Eastern Front was the infantry division. An infantry division was a combat organization of approximately twelve thousand to fifteen thousand men divided into two or three regiments of two to three thousand infantry soldiers each. An infantry division would also contain a series of dedicated supporting units to allow it to independently conduct a range of offensive and defensive operations. Thus, an infantry division might have artillery, anti-tank, reconnaissance, engineers, and anti-aircraft units attached to it. Depending on its mission, tanks or self-propelled guns might also be attached. Furthermore, a division would also include headquarters units, field catering facilities, supplies, signals, medical detachments, and a veterinary unit (if the division depended on horses).

Numbers and structures could, therefore, vary quite significantly. The Soviet divisions were generally smaller, perhaps eight to ten thousand men in total, while the Germans, who had a higher number of supporting troops (such as medical, supplies, transport, and signals), would have thousands more. Divisions that had been fighting for weeks or months could be at half or even less of their official strength. In 1943, the German infantry divisional structure was in the process of reorganization, reducing from three regiments down to two. This was because of the losses suffered in the early four years of fighting and the difficulty in finding replacements. The newly structured division would

---

[1] Glantz, D., and House, J., *The Battle of Kursk*, (University Press of Kansas: Kansas, 1999), pp.337-338.

have fewer troops and would be expected to "do more with less."

The number and types of divisions on the Eastern Front and the number of soldiers in an infantry division varied over the four years of the conflict. Some divisions were wiped out or surrounded and captured, never to be heard of again. Others would be reconstituted and brought back to strength using the remnants of the old division along with new troops. As the war developed, brand-new divisions were created.

At the start of Operation Barbarossa, the Germans had around 140 divisions on the Russian front. The number of Soviet divisions fluctuated between two hundred and three hundred. At any given point in time during this contest, most divisions were below their official strength.

The tank forces of both sides were handled somewhat similarly. They both represented the "mailed fist" of the army. They were able to quickly punch through front lines and operate behind enemy lines. If you wanted to know where the main battles were going to take place, you looked for where the tank units were. They would also form crucial mobile reserves in the event of a crisis.

The Germans operated panzer divisions. Panzer divisions normally had one panzer regiment and two mechanized or motorized infantry regiments, along with supporting arms, including artillery, anti-tank, engineers, signals, and suchlike. There were much fewer panzer divisions than infantry divisions. Seventeen panzer divisions entered Russia in June 1941. Numbers varied according to casualties and the need to conduct operations elsewhere. Panzer divisions also fought in North Africa, Italy, and, later, Western Europe. Panzergrenadier divisions possessed all the attributes of panzer divisions but had fewer tanks. Some units, such as motorized divisions, were upgraded to panzer division status. Others, like the Grossdeutschland infantry regiment, were also upgraded.

Some SS panzergrenadier divisions were effectively panzer divisions simply because of the high number of tanks they possessed. By 1943, if a panzer division had more than two hundred tanks, it was doing very well. Having fewer tanks was far more commonplace. In 1943, the official tank strength for a standard panzer division was 160 tanks.

The Germans brought around 70 percent of their entire Eastern Front tank strength to the Battle of Kursk.[i] The bulk of the German tank

---

[i] 'German Tanks at Kursk,' *The Tank Museum*, 18 July 2107,

force was still made up of the Panzer Mark III, which was approaching obsolescence and had a small 50 mm gun, and the Panzer Mark IV, which, having been regularly upgraded with armor and weapons, was still broadly comparable to the T-34. There were only 150 Tiger tanks available for use at the Battle of Kursk.[i]

On the eve of Kursk, most panzer divisions were still struggling to get to full strength. As an example, the three panzer divisions of the 47th Panzer Corps, part of the 9th Army on the northern shoulder of the salient, had the following tank numbers:

- 20th Panzer Division – 82 tanks
- 9th Panzer Division – 83 tanks
- 2nd Panzer Division – 118 tanks

Some divisions were augmented with additional attached units, like the Grossdeutschland's Panther brigade. The Grossdeutschland in the southern sector is listed as having 132 tanks and 35 assault guns.[ii] With the addition of the specially formed 21st Panzer Brigade, another two hundred Panthers were added for a total of nearly 350 tanks and assault guns. Other independent tank or assault gun units were attached to infantry or panzer divisions as necessary and according to specific tasks. Two to four divisions were grouped into corps, and two to four corps were grouped into armies. A grouping of several armies comprised an army group. The size and strength of German corps, armies, and army groups varied considerably, mainly according to the fortunes of war.

The Soviets no longer used tank divisions, which they had found cumbersome and hard to command during the early stages of the war. They favored tank brigades, consisting of approximately sixty to seventy tanks each. Three tank brigades and a mechanized infantry brigade would form a tank corps consisting of around two hundred tanks. A tank army was made of two tank corps and one mechanized corps, giving a powerful assault force of forty-eight thousand men and five hundred tanks. Infantry and tank armies were grouped into "fronts."

---

https://tankmuseum.org/article/german-tanks-kursk

[i] 'German Tanks at Kursk,' *The Tank Museum*, 18 July 2107, https://tankmuseum.org/article/german-tanks-kursk

[ii] Glantz, D., and House, J., *The Battle of Kursk*, (University Press of Kansas: Kansas, 1999), p.286.

Defenses and Final Preparations

The Soviets knew that Operation Citadel was coming. They knew the location and had a very good sense of timing and German strength. They had received strategic intelligence from the British and their own agents. In and around Kursk, spies, agents, and partisans kept feeding in and updating information. Aerial reconnaissance augmented this flow of information. However, nothing was left to chance. The Soviets began to extensively dig anti-tank ditches, trenches, and other fortifications. Thousands of civilian men and women were forced to dig ditches. Hundreds of thousands of mines were laid—over five thousand per mile of the front. The Soviets prepared three main defensive belts with trenches, ditches, and minefields. Several lines of defense were constructed inside these three main defensive sets.

As Hitler delayed, the Soviets had more time to dig down and further improve their defensive positions with bunkers, barbed wire, and more minefields. Strong points in the farming villages, the woods, and the hilltops were established with a mix of troops—infantry, engineers, anti-tank guns, tanks, and artillery pieces. The blitzkrieg, which had conquered Western Europe and large parts of Russia, provided a stark warning and a strong incentive to avoid complacency. At this point in the war, in the summer of 1943, no army had ever managed to stop a full-scale German blitzkrieg attack dead in its tracks.

The Forces Line Up

The Soviet Central Front, under General Konstantin Rokossovsky, was responsible for defending the northern half of the Kursk bulge, which included Kursk itself. To do this, he had five infantry armies and one tank army, a force of half a million men, and ten thousand artillery pieces. He also had 1,600 tanks and self-propelled guns. Defending the southern half of the bulge was General Nikolai Vatutin's Voronezh Front, which consisted of seven armies, including one tank army. Vatutin commanded 460,000 men, 8,500 artillery pieces, and 1,700 tanks and assault guns. Located to the east, directly behind the Voronezh and Central Fronts, was the Steppe Front, a reserve designed to reinforce the front line, feeding in troops and tanks where needed and participating in counterattacks should the situation allow it. The Steppe Front added another half a million men, 8,500 artillery pieces, and 1,600 tanks. The Bryansk Front, under General Popov, was the next front north of Rokossovsky. It had three infantry armies and one tank army. It would not be involved in the defense of the Kursk salient. Instead, it was being held in readiness to launch its own assault westward, aiming at Orel and Bryansk to hamper the German attack south. Similarly, the Southwestern Font, under General Malinovski, was positioned south of the Voronezh Front and would participate in later counterattacks in the Kharkov area.

From the German perspective, the northern shoulder of the Kursk salient would be attacked by General Walter Model's 9th Army. Part of Army Group Center, the 9th Army comprised two infantry corps and three panzer corps. A battalion of Pz. VI Tiger Tanks (thirty-one tanks) and two detachments of the new heavily armed and armored Elefant self-propelled anti-tank gun (ninety vehicles in total) augmented the assault force. Model had fourteen infantry divisions, six panzer divisions, and three lesser-quality Hungarian divisions (primarily employed on rear area security duties). This gave him about a third of a million men and one thousand tanks and self-propelled guns.

Operations against the southern shoulder were controlled by Army Group South, which would use two armies. The 4th Panzer Army, under General Hermann Hoth, had one infantry corps and two very powerful panzer corps, including the Grossdeutschland division as part of the 48th Panzer Corps and the three SS panzergrenadier divisions that made up the 2nd SS Panzer Corps. Army Detachment Kempf, under General Werner Kempf, had two infantry corps and one panzer corps. Hoth and Kempf, in total, had 350,000 soldiers and 1,700 tanks and self-propelled guns. Army Group South had another panzer corps, the 24th, with two panzer divisions in reserve.

Adolf Hitler continued to vacillate about the dates of the attack. The start date had initially been set at May 4th, 1943. The new Panther tank (whose design had been heavily influenced by the sloping armor of the T-34) was his greatest concern, as he saw it as a key weapon for the coming summer's operations. On May 10th, in Berlin, Heinz Guderian, who was in charge of tank production, explained the situation to Hitler:

"I was summoned to the Chancellery for a discussion on Panther production, since the industry did not think it could complete its programme according to the original schedule. By way of compensation, the industry promised that instead of 250 tanks it would deliver the handsome total of 324 by May 31st... I urged him earnestly to give up the plan for an attack on the Eastern Front."[i]

Operation Citadel was postponed to June 12th. On May 13th, a quarter of a million German soldiers in Tunisia laid down their arms. If that disaster was not bad enough, it opened the prospect of Allied invasions across the Mediterranean, including against Sicily and Italy, potentially knocking Hitler's ally and friend, Benito Mussolini, out of the war. While Hitler again considered canceling the operation completely, Operation Citadel was pushed back to the end of June. The Soviets kept digging. German commanders remained doubtful about the operation.[ii]

Guderian was soon to record more problems with the Panther:

"I spent June 15th worrying about our problem child, the Panther; the track suspension and drive were not right and the optics were also not yet satisfactory. On the next day I told Hitler of my reasons for not wishing to see the Panthers sent into action in the East. They were simply not yet ready to go the front ... Apart from the technical weaknesses of the not yet perfected tanks, neither the crews nor the commanders were by then sufficiently experienced in their handling, while some of them even lacked battle experience."[iii]

On June 18th, the German high command recommended calling off the operation. Hitler decided that the date of the attack would be July 3rd. This would again be changed; the main operation began on July 5th.

It was now the height of summer. The Soviet forces had been brought to a high state of readiness. Extensive intelligence and reconnaissance efforts had told them the time and place of the attack. They had rehearsed their roles and were confident in their abilities, although they were tense and frustrated by the constant alerts. Battlefield defenses had been prepared; there were now six major defensive belts.

On July 1st, Adolf Hitler issued an operational order to be communicated to all soldiers, explaining the importance of the mission. On the same day, the Soviet forces went on full alert.[iv] Over the next

---

[i] Guderian, H., *Panzer Leader,* (Futura: London, 1980), p.308.

[ii] Glantz, D., and House, J., *The Battle of Kursk,* (University Press of Kansas: Kansas, 1999), pp.51-55.

[iii] Guderian, H., *Panzer Leader,* (Futura: London, 1980), p.310.

[iv] Glantz, D., and House, J., *The Battle of Kursk,* (University Press of Kansas: Kansas, 1999), p.78.

couple of days, German assault troops made their way carefully and silently to their forward jumping-off positions. Sporadic skirmishes took place on July 4th, as some German reconnaissance forces probed the first lines of Soviet defenses. A few German prisoners and deserters taken by the Soviets during those hours served to confirm that Operation Citadel would commence before dawn on July 5th. Adolf Hitler's "small foray" was about to begin.

Chapter 5 – The Attack Starts in the North

The Northern Flank

The northern German force that would undertake the assault southward toward Kursk was to be led by the 9th Army under Colonel-General Walter Model. Model was an ardent Nazi who had demonstrated a ruthless approach to getting things done and had performed well enough in the handling of panzer units in the invasion of Russia two years previously. At the start of Operation Barbarossa, he had been in charge of the 3rd Panzer Division and was promoted to take charge of the 41st Panzer Corps in October 1941.

He was not particularly well liked and had a tendency to change plans at a moment's notice. He could be harsh toward

General Walter Model, 9th Army commander, on the front line somewhere in Russia.[5]

his own men and officers and was often careless about casualties. However, he could be flexible and adaptable. In the later stages of the war, he became an expert in conducting mobile defenses. His performance at the gates of Moscow and during the savage fighting in the 1941/42 winter saw him promoted again. He took charge of the 9th Army in January 1942. What's more, he was trusted by Hitler.

By the middle of 1943, the 9th Army had received many replacements and reinforcements. At this point, the 9th Army comprised around 335,000 men, with 21 German and 3 Hungarian divisions. Of these divisions, there were six panzer divisions and one panzergrenadier division.

In theory, the 9th Army could muster an impressive strike force of about six hundred tanks and four hundred self-propelled guns. However, not all of these were of high quality or ready for operations.[i] These armored vehicles were primarily grouped in three separate panzer corps, lined up, west to east against the Soviet front line, as follows: the 46th, 47th, and 41st. Of these panzer corps, the 47th, in the center, was the strongest, comprising three panzer divisions, a panzergrenadier division, and an infantry division. The 46th Panzer Corps did not have any panzer divisions at all and was expected to hold the right flank of the 47th Panzer Corps as it (hopefully) plunged deep into Soviet territory. The precious, new, heavily armored Elefant self-propelled guns had been allocated in their entirety to the 41st Panzer Corps. There were high hopes for the ninety Elefant vehicles, which had been divided into two battalions. On the easternmost shoulder of this northern strike force was the 23rd Infantry Corps, which was to protect the left flank of the advance. This was the starting line-up for the 9th Army.

Model, like many of the German generals contemplating their role in this summer offensive, was skeptical of the operation's necessity, the value of the goal, and the chances of success. He had presented his views to Hitler, arguing that he needed more tanks—the new Panther and Elefant, in particular—so that he could increase his chances of punching through the daunting Soviet defense lines. As General Heinz Guderian recalled in his memoirs from a meeting in early May 1943, "Model had produced information, largely based on air photography, which showed

---

[i] Glantz, D., and House, J., *The Battle of Kursk*, (University Press of Kansas: Kansas, 1999), p.51.

that the Russians were preparing deep and very strong defensive positions in exactly those areas where the attack by the two army groups was to go in ... Model drew the correct deduction from this, namely, that the enemy was counting on our launching this attack and that in order to achieve success we must adopt a fresh tactical approach."[i]

Model's assault concept differed from that of Hoth in the south. Model planned to use his infantry and engineers to move forward first. They would clear away the mines, wire, bunkers, trenches, and strongpoints to create a pathway through which his panzers could be launched as a mobile force. Hoth, on the other hand, decided that the panzers should be used first to batter their way into and through the defensive lines.

But there was another problem for Model. It was becoming clear that, just to his north, in the sector of the German 2nd Panzer Army, the Soviets were planning and preparing for their own offensive westward toward Orel and Bryansk. While Model was expected to be focused on driving his forces southward, he would also be looking anxiously over his left shoulder in fear that a major Soviet attack might be launched behind his back.

In the end, the Soviets struck first. Stalin had received confirmation of the Germans' impending offensive on July 2nd, and all Soviet troops were put on high alert. The Soviets had received several alerts since May, but the Germans had kept postponing. But this time, it was for real. On the evening of July 4th, 1943, Soviet soldiers captured a German engineer in no man's land, the gap between the front lines of both armies attempting to clear the minefields. Under interrogation, he confirmed the timings of the German attack.

With a good sense of the Germans' intentions, locations, movements, and timings, Rokossovsky, the commander of the Central Front facing Model, ordered pre-dawn air attacks followed by artillery barrages at four in the morning of July 5th in order to disrupt German troop concentrations and timings. They were not as effective as hoped. The rigid nature of the Soviet air attacks meant many aircraft were shot down. However, some German deployments faced delays—one or two hours in places. General Zhukov was unimpressed by the efforts of his air force.

---

[i] Guderian, H., *Panzer Leader,* (Futura: London, 1980), pp.306-307.

"It should not be forgotten that the counter-preparation took place at night, as a result of which the air force made an insignificant, and to be quite honest, ineffective contribution; raids on enemy aerodromes at dawn did not fulfil their purpose in any way at all as the German Command had its aircraft in the air by that time to assist its ground troops. Our air force managed to be considerably more effective, striking at tactical battle arrays and enemy columns, which were regrouping during the fighting ... the artillery counter-preparation did inflict heavy losses on the enemy and disorganized the troop control in the course of the offensive but, all the same, we had expected that its impact would be greater."[i]

However, the raids concerned the German commanders and soldiers at the time. Despite their efforts at camouflage and concealment, it was clear that there would be no element of tactical surprise available to give them a battlefield advantage. The fear of their own aircraft being caught and lined up on their airfields, fully fueled and laden with bombs and munitions, was suddenly very real. Nevertheless, by dawn and seemingly largely untroubled by this first blow by the Soviet Air Forces, something in the region of 1,700 German combat aircraft were in the skies over Kursk, seeking to dominate the battlefield.

At 4:30, the Soviet artillery barrage ceased. A German artillery bombardment went ahead and lasted about an hour. At 5:30, German ground troops moved forward, supported by many self-propelled assault guns, which are effectively tanks without turrets. The crucial challenge for the Germans on both the northern and southern fronts was to deal with the thousands of mines. The assault engineers attempted to create paths through the minefields. This proved very difficult, not least because the engineers were often under fire while they worked. Many Soviet mines were enclosed in wooden or cardboard boxes, which made the metal detectors next to useless.

In the German 31st Division's sector of attack, the engineers went in daylight over flat ground, covered by the Tiger tanks of the 505th Battalion, holding back in the rear with their long-range 88 mm guns. Without cover, the engineers soon came under mortar and artillery fire and suffered heavy casualties. After two hours of hazardous work, they managed to open some lanes in the minefields. The soldiers of the 23rd

---

[i] Zhukov, G., *Reminiscences and Reflections*, (Progress Publishers: Moscow, 1985). p.183.

Infantry Corps on the easternmost edge of Model's attack launched their own attacks, intending mainly to confuse and distract the Soviets from the main push by the 41st and 47th Panzer Corps. They managed an advance of about a mile into the Soviets' first defensive belt before grinding to a halt under the weight of firepower. The Soviets even managed a few local counterattacks of their own.

Other high-tech solutions for clearing mines were brought into action. Two small crewless remote-controlled armored vehicle types—the Goliath and the Borgward BIV—which were packed full of explosives, were driven into the minefields and then detonated, exploding many mines in the process.[i] The BIVs were also used to support the advance of the Elefant self-propelled guns of the 653rd Heavy Panzerjäger Battalion operating on the front of the 86th Infantry Division. The slow-moving armored fortresses were saturated with heavy artillery fire. The shells were not always damaging to the heavily armored vehicles, but the dust and smoke considerably restricted visibility.

And the Elefants took a battering. Not all of them were destroyed, but many had to be abandoned when they broke down or suffered damage, such as a track blown off by a mine that could not be repaired in the middle of the battlefield. One of the great blunders in the design of the Elefant was rapidly exposed in the face of real combat against a brave enemy. Although the Elefants undoubtedly had a powerful anti-tank gun and thick armor, they had no machine guns that could fend off infantry attacks armed with anti-tank rifles, grenades, and even simple Molotov cocktail petrol bombs. This meant that while the Elefants could certainly punch through a Soviet defense line, if their infantry support were unable to keep up, they were highly vulnerable to small groups of Soviet infantry and engineers who stalked the battlefield or lurked in trenches and bushes amidst the smoke and confusion.

At the start of the morning, the 653rd Heavy Panzerjäger Battalion had forty-nine operational vehicles. By five o'clock that evening, they were down to twelve. Most of the losses had been to mines.[ii]

---

[i] The descendants of these vehicles can be seen in operations in 2024 in the war between Russia and Ukraine.

[ii] Remson, A., and Anderson, D., 'Mine and Countermine Operations in the battle of Kursk, 25 Apr. 2000, p.39.

Model's infantry pushed forward, desperately trying to open gaps for the panzers to have a clear ride. However, the smoke and dust made it hard to identify cleared paths, and tanks and armored vehicles regularly stumbled into mined areas despite the efforts of the engineers to clear and mark paths.

The main attack by the 41st and 47th Panzer Corps had some successes in the vicinity of the large railway town of Ponyri on the eastern flank. The panzers were well supported by aircraft and artillery and managed advances in some places up to three miles. They also captured the well-defended village of Bobrik, ten miles west of Ponyri. The fighting was intense and set the tone for the combat in both the north and south sectors of the Battle of Kursk.

Here is an eyewitness account from a Soviet soldier in the Soviet 29th Corps sector (opposite the German 41st Panzer Corps) facing an attack by the German 18th Panzer Division a few miles northwest of Ponyri:

"The sky blackened from smoke and heat. The acrid gases from the exploding shells and mines blinded the eyes. The soldiers were deafened by the thunder of guns and mortars and the creaking of tracks ... As the Germans neared the forward edge, anti-tank artillery and anti-tank rifles opened direct fire on their tanks. Mortar and machine-gun fire concentrated on the enemy infantry ... the penetrating enemy tanks began blowing up in the minefields. More and more frequently the enemy infantry began to hit the dirt. Only by 09.00 hours did the enemy succeed in penetrating in the dispositions of ... 81st Rifle Division and ... 15th Rifle Division."[i]

---

[i] Glantz, D., and House, J., *The Battle of Kursk*, (University Press of Kansas: Kansas, 1999), p.88.

A Soviet two-man crew operate an anti-tank rifle under fire. These weapons stood no chance of penetrating a tank's frontal armor but could damage trucks, armored personnel carriers, and the tracks of tanks.[6]

The fighting was bitter and at close range. Soviet infantry scrambled onto German vehicles to assault them with grenades and Molotov cocktails. The German soldiers were supported by Elefants and Tiger tanks.

Ponyri was a key objective for the Germans, but it was heavily defended. As some Soviet forces in the area crumbled under the powerful German attack, General Rokossovsky dispatched reinforcements to prop up the defense, sending a tank brigade and a self-propelled artillery regiment. The Soviets repelled four German attacks but were compelled to retreat during the fifth attack.

On the western flank of the German attack, the 46th Panzer Corps, which did not have any panzer divisions but had some support from Tiger tanks, made minimal progress with its 7th and 31st Infantry Divisions. An attack by the 258th Division fared badly and was judged to have "ground to a halt after only minimal gains."[i]

---

[i] Glantz, D., and House, J., *The Battle of Kursk*, (University Press of Kansas: Kansas, 1999), p.89.

This was largely how the first few days on the northern front played out. The Soviets were well prepared. The Germans had a powerful and motivated force, but they struggled to make headway against the mines, dug-in soldiers, and heavy Soviet artillery barrages.

The Germans learned two things over the first days of the attack. The Soviets were not retreating in the face of German armored attacks, and there was no evidence that the Soviets had been taken by surprise.[i]

The fighting intensified. German progress was slow, and the Soviet resistance was stiff. Pinning his hopes on the 47th Panzer Corps in the center, Model threw in the 2nd and 9th Panzer Divisions. Again, progress was made; the additional panzer power advanced the Germans another three miles or so, getting closer to the Soviets' second defensive belt. Here, the battle was less about tank against tank but more about tank against mines. The Soviets had two objectives with the mines: to slow the Germans and to inflict casualties. They did this very effectively.[ii]

By the end of July 5th, the Germans had captured a small slice of land approximately five miles by ten miles, but it came at great cost. Some reports suggested that two hundred of the initially available three hundred German tanks and self-propelled guns were no longer operational. This did not mean they were all destroyed. Engineers worked furiously to retrieve the damaged vehicles from a dangerous battlefield and make hasty repairs just behind the front line.

"Although some of these vehicles could be repaired at night, Model had lost at least 20 percent of his total armored striking power on the first day, when his troops were at their strongest."[iii]

Modal was disappointed by the seven to eight miles the Germans had advanced. Rokossovsky continued to bring up reinforcements and conduct counterattacks. By the evening of July 5th, he had prepared up to 750 tanks and self-propelled guns for fresh attacks on the following day. Some of the Soviet counterattacks were poorly prepared. Tank units were thrown in without the opportunity to conduct reconnaissance.

---

[i] Glantz, D., and House, J., *The Battle of Kursk*, (University Press of Kansas: Kansas, 1999), pp.90-81.

[ii] Remson, A., and Anderson, D., 'Mine and Countermine Operations in the battle of Kursk, 25 Apr. 2000, p.41.

[iii] Glantz, D., and House, J., *The Battle of Kursk*, (University Press of Kansas: Kansas, 1999), p.91.

Many units had to get in place over a short night of only a few hours of darkness (dawn was around 4:30 in early July). Less than half of the tanks were where they were supposed to be when the sun rose.

On July 6th, the 46th Panzer Division had to repel attacks by the Soviet 19th Tank Corps (with about 150 tanks) and was only then able to move forward. The 2nd Panzer Division of the 47th Panzer Corps was hit by attacks from two Soviet infantry divisions supported by two Soviet tank corps (with well over three hundred tanks). No significant progress was made by the Germans. The reserves of the 9th Army had been sucked in for no gain.

Rokossovsky's counterattacks were not sophisticated in intent or delivery. They did not inflict decisive damage on the Germans, and they certainly did not cause the Germans to retreat. However, he had a lot of troops that he could throw into this confused fighting, and they caused losses and delays that the Germans could not afford. Kursk was still forty miles away, and German forward progress was now being measured in hundreds of yards.

On July 7th, the intense fighting continued. Rokossovsky sent in more counterattacks, and the Germans found themselves having to respond to these rather than being able to initiate their own operations. Soviet casualties were high, though. Near the village of Butyrka, the German 505th Heavy Tiger Tank Battalion managed to ambush one of these large-scale Soviet tank attacks. The 107th Soviet Tank Brigade of the 16th Tank Corps was savaged, losing forty-six of its fifty tanks. Another tank brigade in support, the 164th, lost another twenty-three tanks.

"Thus the most that the first Soviet counterattack achieved was to delay the German advance for another day. By nightfall, the attacking tanks of the 2nd Tank Army no longer represented a cohesive armored force. Committed in piecemeal fashion, they now fought desperate fragmented battles in support of the hard-pressed Soviet infantry. Soon [General] Rodin would replicate this unfortunate use of Rokossovsky's precious armor by committing General Sinenko's 3rd Tank Corps into battle, again in piecemeal fashion."[i]

However clumsy and costly Rokossovsky's approach was, General Model could not afford another day of delay. On July 6th, his troops had

---

[i] Glantz, D., and House, J., *The Battle of Kursk*, (University Press of Kansas: Kansas, 1999), p.93.

only advanced half the distance that they had advanced the day before. He would conduct regular evening meetings with his commanders to prepare for the next day. He was formulating much more pragmatic and limited objectives for the next day's fighting. Model sought to achieve a few miles of advance rather than the sweeping blitzkrieg maneuvers of 1941 and 1942. Another one of Model's reserve formations—the 4th Panzer Division—was pushed into the fray.

The 41st Panzer Corps threw the 18th Panzer Division and the 86th and 292nd Infantry into action at Ponyri in an attempt to envelop the town on both sides. The battle for Ponyri was becoming increasingly costly and protracted. Its railway station and yards, along with a tractor plant and other industrial areas, were stubbornly held by the Soviets. A village schoolhouse and a water tower were defended fanatically. The town eventually became nicknamed "Little Stalingrad" by the weary German grenadiers. There was to be no German breakthrough at Ponyri.

Battle casualties continued to increase. The 505th Heavy Tiger Tank Battalion, which was so crucial to the operations of the otherwise panzerless divisions of the 46th Panzer Corps, reported on July 7th that it had two tanks destroyed (out of a total of thirty-one in the battalion) but that it had as many as twenty-five damaged and requiring repair. Well over half of these losses were attributed to mine damage.[i] The 47th Panzer Corps began to change its tactics in order to address this major problem, ordering that mine-clearing engineers in armored personnel carriers should accompany each Tiger company when they advanced.

The 9th Army's assault momentum was clearly flagging. No significant breakthroughs or advances had been made by any of Model's divisions. He called a conference with his corps commanders on July 8th in order to review the situation, discuss tactics, and assess what might still be achievable. It did not appear that reaching Kursk fell into this category. Infantry and tank losses had been significant.

"Of the more than 700 tanks in the panzer divisions of the 9th Army on July 5, less than half were operational three days later. Some units had suffered crippling losses. Heavy Panzerjäger Battalion 653, for example, which began July 5 with 45 Ferdinands [Elefants], had no vehicles operational on July 8 and ceased combat operations for a

---

[i] Remson, A., and Anderson, D., 'Mine and Countermine Operations in the battle of Kursk, 25 Apr. 2000, p.52

'recovery day.'"[i]

In three days, the 9th Army had advanced little more than ten miles, penetrating the first Soviet defense line and reaching—but not penetrating—the second defense line. The troops were exhausted after three or four days of continuous operations. The Soviet defenses remained strong, and Russian reinforcements continued to flow into the battle area.

Nevertheless, the 9th Army made one more significant effort. From July 8th to 10th, the 47th Panzer Corps flung three panzer and panzergrenadier divisions into action in and around the small village of Teploe. It was another brutal back-and-forth action with high casualties for little gain. Heavy Soviet artillery pinned down the German infantry as soon as they moved forward. Although some German tanks and infantry broke through, they were quickly repelled by Soviet counterattacks. The cycle of small German gains and bitter counterattacks was repeated several times.

There is only so much that flesh can do against fast-moving metal. By July 10th, it was clear to Model, his commanders, and his soldiers that an advance was simply not possible.

"Losses among the German soldiers were mounting so rapidly that the Wehrmacht assaults almost visibly began to break down in the field of battle."[ii]

No German advances were recorded at all on July 10th.

On July 12th, Model was still regrouping and looking to continue the attacks. However, he was too late and was overtaken by events to his north. On that day, General Popov launched Operation Kutuzov, a massive attack westward toward Bryansk. This struck the German 2nd Panzer Army, the tank army largely without any tanks, immediately north of Model's 9th Army.

To a large extent, this Soviet attack had been anticipated. German intelligence had been monitoring troop buildups for some time. Army Group Center's commander, Field Marshal Gunther von Kluge, and Model had contingency plans in place. But Operation Kutuzov, with a

---

[i] Remson, A., and Anderson, D., 'Mine and Countermine Operations in the battle of Kursk, 25 Apr. 2000, p.52

[ii] Caidin, M., *The Tigers Are Burning*, (Pinnacle Books, Los Angeles, 1980), p.214.

million Soviet soldiers and 2,500 tanks, posed a new set of challenges for the Germans. It meant an immediate end to the German combat operations in the northern sector of the Kursk offensive. Even more critically, it threatened German forces in the Orel region and Model's 9th Army as well. Model immediately had to start pulling precious panzer units off the battlefield and turn them northward, including the 9th Panzer Division and the 10th Panzergrenadier Division.

For this and other strategic reasons (as we shall see), Hitler effectively brought Operation Citadel to a halt after this. Kursk would not fall to the German Army.

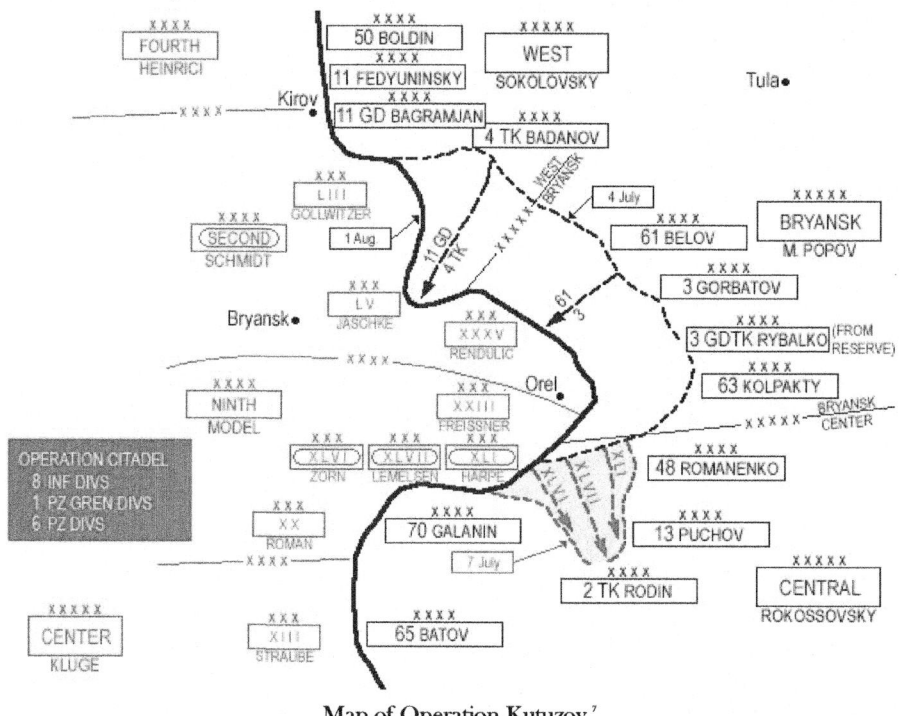

Map of Operation Kutuzov.[7]

Chapter 6 – The Attack on the Southern Flank

Let's turn to the southern part of the German operations in Kursk. Relatively speaking, it fared more successfully due to the greater number of panzer units and the strategic misjudgment of Soviet commanders. The Russians had anticipated that the strongest German blow would come from the north and had based their reserves accordingly. This was one of the reasons why Model's 9th Army struggled to break through Soviet defenses.

Field Marshal Erich von Manstein's Army Group South was responsible for the southern drive into the Kursk salient. This was the officially phrased order that von Manstein had received:

"With concentrated forces, Army Group South breaks out to the west of the Belgorod area, advances on a line Prilepy-Oboyan to the east and makes contact with Army Group Center near Kursk. The attack is to be screened to the east and west."[i]

The main force von Manstein assigned to the task was the 4th Panzer Army, comprising three corps—the 52nd Infantry Corps on the western flank, the 48th Panzer Corps in the center, and the 2nd SS Panzer Corps on the eastern flank. Supporting the 4th Panzer Army to the southeast in the Belgorod area was another army-sized formation, Army Detachment

---

[i] Remson, A., and Anderson, D., 'Mine and Countermine Operations in the battle of Kursk, 25 Apr. 2000, p.56

Kempf, named after its commander, General Werner Kempf. Kempf had a powerful force, including the 3rd Panzer Corps, which would play a prominent role in the fighting. However, Kempf's force was located to the south of the 2nd SS Panzer Corps, meaning that the 3rd Panzer Corps frequently had to travel much farther in order to keep up with them.

Like Model's task, the plan was relatively straightforward: punch a hole through the Soviet defense lines and drive on to Kursk. The 4th Panzer Army's goal initially was Oboyan, located thirty miles from their starting positions, and then Kursk, which was another thirty-five miles directly north. To do this, the Germans would need to secure bridgeheads over the Psel River.

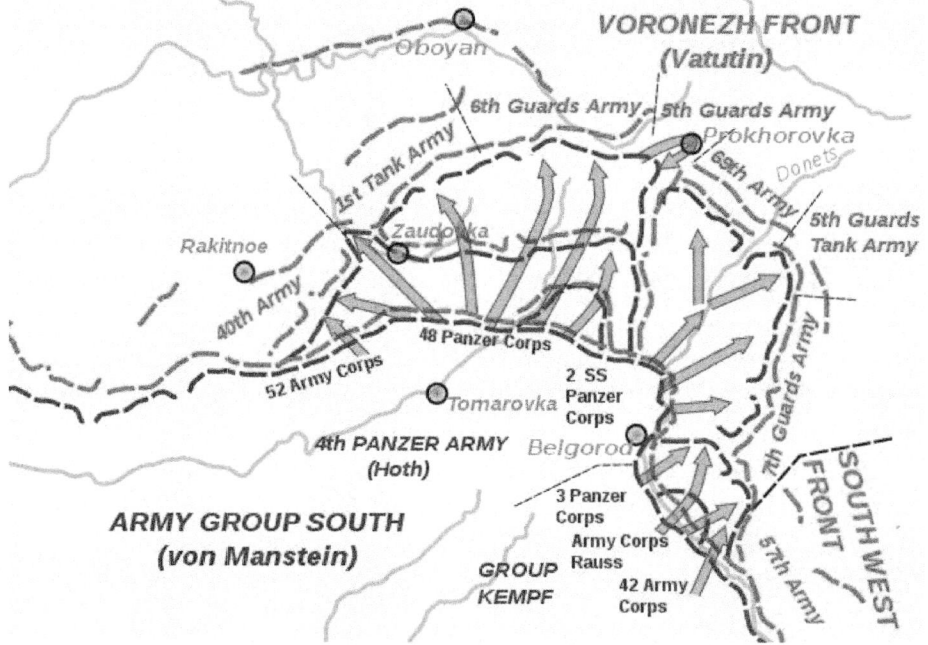

Von Manstein's corps dispositions on the eve of the battle. Oboyan, the initial target, is at the top of the map. Kursk is another thirty-five miles from Oboyan.[8]

The southern attacks were meant to be conducted simultaneously with the northern thrust. At the local level, there was some flexibility regarding timings. Some operations began on July 4th. A major German artillery barrage took place in the afternoon of July 4th, supported by attacks from one hundred Ju 87 "Stuka" dive bombers. Engineers in some sectors were sent ahead early to lift as many mines as possible; some had been working in no man's land since July 3rd, trying to clear paths for the panzers and the assault troops. The Grossdeutschland

Division launched some early infantry-only operations to seize some high ground to their front that would allow better observation of the Soviet positions.

Some of the attacks were also delayed a few hours for various reasons. A handful of captured Germans and deserters gave the timings to the Soviets, who were then anticipating a major attack to begin between July 3rd and July 6th. There was to be no chance of any tactical surprise: the Soviets were ready and waiting.

Amongst the panzer divisions, the tactics for the advance were left to the lower-level tank commanders themselves. In many cases, the heavier tanks, such as the Tigers, were chosen to lead. This was known as the "Panzerkeil" (armored arrow), named after the shape of the formation. Heavy tanks—preferably Tigers—were to be placed at the tip of the advance. Medium tanks would be fanned out on either side of the heavy tanks, and the lighter tanks and commanders' vehicles were tucked away at the rear or the middle. This had the advantage of protecting the less well-armored tanks, such as the Panzer Mark III. The flanks of the force would be screened and protected by anti-tank guns. On the downside, this meant that the Tigers would be the first to face the full weight of Soviet tank and artillery fire, often at very close range.

As the Germans moved forward, they began to encounter the same problems that were facing Model's 9th Army. Soviet artillery fire was intense, and resistance generally was fierce. Despite the blistering heat of high summer in central Russia, there were heavy localized rainstorms from July 4th to July 5th. These turned paths into mud. Streams and ravines that had previously looked traversable were now hard to negotiate, particularly for the trucks and other wheeled vehicles, and some were suddenly impassable, needing bridging equipment if available. It became commonplace during the next two weeks of the operation for German supply trucks to become bogged down, making resupply of food, fuel, and ammunition another major headache for the German commanders.

The sheer volume of mines on the battlefield in front of the Soviet defensive positions also came as a shock and was a problem that was never entirely resolved by the Germans. The mine-clearing engineers of the Grossdeutschland Division reported that they had lifted 2,700 mines in a 5-hour period. These cheap and easy-to-deploy devices played critical roles in slowing the advance of the 4th Panzer Army.

"In spite of the clearing that had been done during the night, the Germans were still hampered by mines. As one participant put it, 'the damned things were everywhere!' One artillery battalion commander had two vehicles blown up under him during the advance, a battery commander was severely wounded by a mine, and the battalion commander of the 3rd battalion of the Panzer Fusilier Regiment Grossdeutschland lost a leg to a mine. Consequently, 'Everyone moved through the terrain slowly with extreme caution.'"[i]

Heavy German artillery bombardments were delivered at four in the morning on July 5th. An hour later, all the panzer corps were at least trying to move forward.

The 48th Panzer Corps (the 3rd and 11th Panzer Divisions, the Grossdeutschland Panzergrenadier Division, and the 332nd Infantry Division) quickly found itself in difficulty, both from the mines and the conditions of the very muddy roads. All of the divisions reported delays. The Grossdeutschland Division struggled to get over an anti-tank ditch and a ravine they had encountered, both of which were full of water. The men would not cross this until July 6th. The division reported losing five self-propelled guns and twenty tanks on the 5th.

The performance of the two hundred Panther tanks of the Grossdeutschland division's 21st Panzer Brigade was less than impressive. In a couple of days, it had lost around forty of the precious vehicles to the mud, mines, and mechanical failures.

However, the corps managed to penetrate the first Soviet defensive line, with advances of up to three miles reported. The 3rd Panzer Division, in particular, made some deeper penetrations into the Soviet positions, giving some cause for optimism amidst the artillery, mines, and mud.

The 2nd SS Panzer Corps also performed well on the first few days, breaking through the first line of defense and moving several miles forward. Its men started to probe into the second line of Soviet positions. The corps had benefited from being the priority for the Luftwaffe; almost all the ground support air power was being used to assist the SS divisions.

---

[i] Remson, A., and Anderson, D., 'Mine and Countermine Operations in the battle of Kursk, 25 Apr. 2000, pp.58-59.

There were powerful Soviet counterattacks, even at this early stage, from groups of thirty, forty, or fifty tanks. Although these attacks were repelled and at some cost to the Soviets, these Soviet punches delayed German operations and forced the Germans to cede the initiative to address these threats. As a result, they quickly lost forward momentum.[j]

Army Detachment Kempf, south of Belgorod, also struggled early on to get into its stride against powerful Soviet counterattacks from a Guards elite rifle corps, tank brigades, and heavy self-propelled guns. The 3rd Panzer Corps struggled with a river crossing and the tricky task of getting all its tanks over a bridge.

The SU-122 self-propelled gun in 1943—essentially a T-34 tank chassis without a turret but packing a powerful 122 mm gun that could threaten even Tiger tanks. Other variants of this weapon system employed 85 mm or 152 mm guns.[9]

Despite the challenges and setbacks the Germans encountered, the advances made by the 4th Panzer Army from July 4th to July 6th were of considerable concern to General Vatutin, commander of the Voronezh Front. He asked for reinforcements. Stavka, the Soviet high command, had been monitoring developments very closely and was prompt to respond, perhaps appreciating that the south appeared to be the main German effort. In addition to new infantry units, four entire tank corps

---

[j] Remson, A., and Anderson, D., 'Mine and Countermine Operations in the battle of Kursk, 25 Apr. 2000, p.71.

were sent forward, arriving on July 7th. Each tank corps comprised around 150 to 200 tanks and was, therefore, the rough equivalent of a full-strength panzer division.

Two other factors were also brought into play to assist the defenders. The Soviet Air Forces were refocused and concentrated on the southern front. The 5th Guards Tank Army, under General Rotmistrov, on the Steppe Front reserve to the east, was put on notice to move forward and be prepared to advance against the eastern flank of the 2nd SS Panzer Corps as they pushed north. The 5th Guards Tank Army would become famous at the Battle of Prokhorovka in less than a week's time.

Von Manstein focused on getting his panzer forces to exploit the gaps in the second defense line and then to push up to and into the third line. While this was underway, it was essential that the panzer divisions' western and eastern flanks were protected as they moved north. If powerful Soviet tank forces were able to force their way around the sides, the Germans could be in real trouble.

The 48th Panzer Corps would always find this difficult. The intention had been to use the 332nd Infantry Division of the corps to guard the western flank and to ensure that the 52nd Infantry Corps, even farther to the west, was keeping up with the advance. It was crucial that the panzer divisions concentrated on punching through toward Oboyan.

To the German soldiers and tank crews faced with crossing the Pena River while under fire, the Soviet resistance seemed even tougher than before. Again, the Panther brigade suffered more losses to a well-concealed minefield. By the early evening, the brigade was down to only forty tanks. Several Tiger tanks were also knocked out, and all three panzer divisions of the corps were reduced to a crawl amidst minefields, heavy defensive fire from the Soviets, and numerous counterattacks from Soviet tank formations. Attacks and counterattacks lasted several hours, with little to show on the German side other than knocked-out vehicles and high casualties.

With the Soviets seeing the thrust of the 48th Panzer Corps as the Germans' main effort, the 2nd SS Panzer Corps, on the right of the 48th Panzer Corps, was able to make a bit more progress and had, initially at least, a slightly easier ride. The 1st Leibstandarte (literally "Lifeguards") Adolf Hitler Panzer Division moved forward about three miles, and the 2nd Das Reich Division advanced about five miles in the morning until it finally met some serious resistance. Russian tank attacks were beaten off.

By the end of the day, the SS troops had advanced over ten kilometers. However, they were still far from the third Soviet defensive belt.[i]

The SS panzer forces, which met less resistance, continued to push northeast along the road toward Prokhorovka. However, this was *northeast*, not the desired northerly direction toward Oboyan. Army Detachment Kempf made little progress and was still struggling to get into a position to protect the eastern flank of the 2nd SS Panzer Corps. The SS soldiers would have to look after their own for the moment.

The Air War over Kursk

The war in the air over the Kursk battlefields was very active, with thousands of sorties flown by both sides. Although the Soviets benefited numerically—they had many more aircraft to throw into the fight—the superior Luftwaffe aircraft and tactics were more than enough to inflict severe losses on the Soviet Air Forces.

Many German air units from across Russia were drafted to provide ground support for the fighting troops or to combat the increasing number of Soviet aircraft. The marauding Soviet Sturmovik IL-2 ground attack aircraft was increasingly feared and respected by the German Army.

The Luftwaffe's role in supporting troops on the ground was critical. One of the reconnaissance battalions of the 48th Panzer Corps made the following entry into its war diary:

"With admiration we watch the Stukas attacking the Russian tanks uninterruptedly and with wonderful precision. Squadron after Squadron of Stukas come over to drop their deadly eggs on the Russian armor. Dazzling white flames indicate that another enemy tank has 'brewed up'. This happens again and again."[ii]

July 5th reportedly saw the largest amount of aerial combat over the Russian front. Luftwaffe pilots claimed to have shot down 432 Soviet aircraft.[iii] However, the Luftwaffe was starting to struggle and could not always sustain its operations. Its own losses meant that it could not always guarantee the crucial air superiority that would protect the armored

---

[i] Remson, A., and Anderson, D., 'Mine and Countermine Operations in the battle of Kursk, 25 Apr. 2000, p.77.

[ii] Mellenthin, F. von, *Panzer Battles*, (Futura Publications Ltd: London, 1979), p.273.

[iii] Weal, J., *Jagdgeschwader 52: The Experten*, (Osprey Publishing: Oxford, 2004), p.94.

advances. The strain of the combat and the extended hours of operations took their toll. Fighter ace Erich Hartmann reported flying for fifteen hours on July 5th, shooting down four Soviet aircraft. On July 7th, he became an "ace in a day" by shooting down eight Soviet aircraft, five of which were believed to be Sturmoviks.[i] In addition, resupply columns would struggle at points to negotiate boggy ground and muddy tracks. Some Luftwaffe operations were delayed or canceled because the fuel was not available in time and in sufficient quantities.

There was another interesting aerial feature of note, an innovation that has expanded and developed throughout the decades that followed. At this point in the war, the legendary Ju 87 Stuka dive bomber was old and slow. It was struggling to survive against the Allies in North Africa, Tunisia, Italy, and, from mid-1944 onward, France and northwest Europe. Highly advanced American and British aircraft, such as the Mustang and the Spitfire, would make short work of them. More or less obsolete, by 1943, the bulk of the Stukas were deployed on the Russian front—over 80 percent of them—where the Soviet Air Forces were less of a threat.[ii]

Looking for new tactics to enhance close air support and to deal with the hundreds of Soviet armored vehicles roaming the battlefield, by 1943, the Luftwaffe had established an experimental air unit that had been testing the fitting of 30 mm, 37 mm, and even 75 mm guns onto Stukas and also the twin-engine Henschel HS-109 aircraft as an anti-tank weapon.

This had real potential to give new life to the Stuka dive bombers. Here, on the flat Russian steppe and generally against poor-quality Soviet opposition, the Stukas learned to fly straight and low, aiming against the thinner rear armor of the turrets and engine decks of the Soviet tanks. This could often be extremely effective and disrupt Soviet armored attacks and inflict great loss. The veteran and highly decorated German Stuka pilot Hans-Ulrich Rudel had been involved in these trials. His squadron was sent to Kursk at short notice to support the panzer

---

[i] See a table in Annex 1 listing all of Erich Hartmann's claimed kills from November 5th, 1942, to May 8th, 1945, Hind, C., & Nicolaides, A. (2020). Ace of Aces: Erich Hartmann the Blond Knight of Germany. Open Journal of Social Sciences, 8, 383-406. https://doi.org/10.4236/jss.2020.83034.

[ii] Murray, W., 'Strategy for Defeat: The Luftwaffe, 1933-1945,' *Air University Press*, Jan. 1983, p.158.

divisions.[i] He recalled the moment when he remembered the experimental unit and the Kanonenvogel—the cannon birds.

"The sight of these masses of tanks reminds me of my cannon-carrying aircraft of the experimental unit, which I have brought with me from the Crimea. With this enormous target of enemy tanks it should be possible to try it out ... In the first attack four tanks explode under the hammer blows of my cannons; by the evening the total rises to twelve ... in this aircraft we possess a weapon which can speedily be employed everywhere and is capable of dealing successfully with the formidable numbers of Soviet tanks. There is great rejoicing in the flight, the squadron, the wing and the group ... a signal is immediately sent to all sections of the anti-tank experimental unit, asking for all serviceable aircraft to be flown here at once with crews. So the anti-tank flight is formed. For operational purposes it is under my command."[ii]

A Stuka Ju 87G, in late June 1943, believed to be that of flying ace Hans-Ulrich Rudel. Note the two powerful 37 mm cannons fitted under the wings. Also, on the engine cowling, one tank "kill" has already been painted up.[10]

---

[i] As a point of interest, Hans-Ulrich Rudel's "tank busting" expertise was later called upon by the United States government. In the 1970s he was interviewed by the Department of Defence, which was designing what would become the A-10 ground attack aircraft.

[ii] Rudel, H., *Stuka Pilot*, (Ballantine Books: New York, 1958), p. 106.

However, at Kursk, the Henschel HS-129 aircraft were credited with the first single-handed defeat of a ground armored unit, the Soviet 2nd Guards Tank Corps. Four squadrons of HS-120, mounting a 30 mm cannon, swooped in to attack, destroying many and dispersing even more as the tanks sought cover. The Soviets became more inclined to use nighttime movements after this lethal display of airpower.[i]

Henschel HS-129B in the United States after the war.[ii]

48th Panzer Corps Grinds to a Halt

On July 7th, the Grossdeutschland Division finally had success. One of their attacks caused the Russian forces to break and retreat quickly. In doing so, they suffered heavily from German artillery fire. The panzers pushed aggressively forward and made some progress. There was a real expectation of a breakthrough. The grenadier regiment of the Grossdeutschland reported having taken the key village of Verchopenje, and the route north was wide open. An improvised, highly mobile battle group of reconnaissance troops and assault guns was hastily assembled and sent forward to the north of the village of Novosselovka to take advantage of what seemed to be a significant breach of the Soviet lines.

When the battle group met up with the grenadiers in what they all thought was Verchopenje and started to confer, they began to realize that they were not in the right place. In the fog and confusion of the battle, a map-reading error had led some of the troops to believe they were much farther north than they actually were. In reality, they were in the village of Gremutshy, about seven miles south of Novosselovka. There was to be no breakthrough.[ii]

---

[i] Glantz, D., and House, J., *The Battle of Kursk*, (University Press of Kansas: Kansas, 1999), p.135.

[ii] Mellenthin, F. von, *Panzer Battles*, (Futura Publications Ltd: London, 1979), p.270.

Grenadiers of the Grossdeutschland Division hitch a ride on a StuG Mk. III assault gun, July 1943.[12]

The pressure was mounting to achieve forward momentum, but Soviet resistance was still fearsome. The 3rd Panzer Division, which was on the left, was held up. The 11th Panzer Division, on the right, was just about keeping up with Grossdeutschland in the center. The Grossdeutschland battle groups had to abandon a northern move and pivot west to assist the 3rd Panzer Division, which was dealing with multiple Soviet armored counterattacks. Seven tank attacks were repulsed. Twenty-one T-34 tanks were reported as knocked out. Between the two divisions, the front was stabilized. The Soviets were dealt serious losses, but the Germans did not move any farther forward.

Friedrich von Mellenthin was serving as the chief of staff for the 48th Panzer Corps throughout the Battle of Kursk and had an excellent perspective of the fortunes of war on the southern flank. In his memoirs after the war, he recorded his view that July 8th was the culminating point for the corps.

"It could no longer be doubted that the back of the German attack had been broken and its momentum gone ... The slow progress of the southern pincer was disappointing, but we had in fact done much better than our comrades on the northern flank of the salient."[i]

---

[i] Mellenthin, F. von, *Panzer Battles*, (Futura Publications Ltd: London, 1979), p.271.

On July 9th, the corps attempted to move forward again, but the 3rd Panzer and 11th Panzer both quickly stalled without much progress. The troops were exhausted after five days of continuous action. Frustration grew, as the Grossdeutschland Division was further prevented from attacking north because of Soviet counterattacks. This time, the division had to turn to the south and southwest in order to clear out pockets of resistance and give more assistance to the 3rd Panzer Division.

On July 11th, the 3rd Panzer Division was ordered to relieve the Grossdeutschland Division so that Grossdeutschland could launch an attack northward. The exchange took place on the night of July 11th. As von Mellenthin noted, July 12th was the first time the Grossdeutschland Division had been able to regroup, concentrate its forces, and replenish its ammunition and fuel. Frantic repairs were carried out through the night in order to get every possible vehicle ready for new and hopefully decisive operations.

On the morning of July 13th, the Grossdeutschland reconnaissance battalion started patrolling to the north in anticipation of the next forward thrust. However, the order for a full attack did not come. Instead, there were other reports indicating that the 11th Panzer Division to the east and the 2nd SS Panzer Corps farther east were having problems.

Orders finally came in; they were delivered personally by the 48th Panzer Corps commander, Otto von Knobelsdorff. There would be no attack north. Instead, for the second time, the division was urgently required to move west to assist the 3rd Panzer Division, which had been pushed off a key hilltop and was being attacked from the north and west.

The joint efforts of the 3rd Panzer and the Grossdeutschland Divisions again rectified the situation and inflicted heavy losses on the Soviets, but both panzer divisions were very weak, needing rest and refitting. The 48th Panzer Corps would make no more attempts to drive forward, and Operation Citadel was drawing to a close as "a complete and most regrettable failure."[i]

A few days later, the Grossdeutschland Division was pulled out of the line and sent north to assist with the 9th Army's desperate defense against the Soviets' major offensive toward Orel. By July 23rd, the 4th Panzer Army was more or less back at its pre-July 4th starting point.

---

[i] Mellenthin, F. von, *Panzer Battles*, (Futura Publications Ltd: London, 1979), p.277.

Chapter 7 – Prokhorovka: The Greatest Ever Tank Battle?

Operation Citadel was clearly faltering and, with the benefit of hindsight, was drawing to a close. However, there is one more chapter to be told: the story of the operations of the 2nd SS Panzer Corps and the 5th Guards Tank Army and the intense battle for control of a small railway station on the eastern edge of the 4th Panzer Army's drive northward. The action on July 12th, 1943, is legendary, controversial, intensely debated, and highly mythologized. For many, it is still known as the greatest tank battle of all time.

Let's briefly refresh our understanding of the plans and developments in the eastern part of the southern sector. The main punch from the 4th Panzer Army in the south came from the 48th Panzer Corps and 2nd SS Panzer Corps, which were standing shoulder to shoulder and aiming to head for Oboyan and then Kursk. Because of the intense nature of the Soviet resistance and the terrain, the 2nd SS Panzer Corps' direction of attack, which forced back the Soviet 6th Guards Army, was never entirely northward. Instead, the Germans headed in a northeasterly direction with the intention of turning north when and where possible. Here are the series of dilemmas that General Hausser's SS divisions now faced, as described by David Glantz and Jonathan House, two American military experts on the Battle of Kursk:

"With the 6th Guards Army's second defensive belt now punctured, the II SS Panzer Corps had an open route open to the northeast, with only a motorized brigade (the 6th Guards) of Kravchenko's shaken tank corps to their front. It was an opportunity, however, that Hausser and his corps could not exploit. First his orders were to advance north to [Oboyan], not to Prokhorovka in the northeast ... Second ... he had no choice but to defend those flanks until infantry arrived to permit his armor to resume its headlong advance. In the meantime, Hausser instinctively permitted his forces to continue marching along the line of least resistance ... his advanced elements pushed farther north along the road to Prokhorovka."[i]

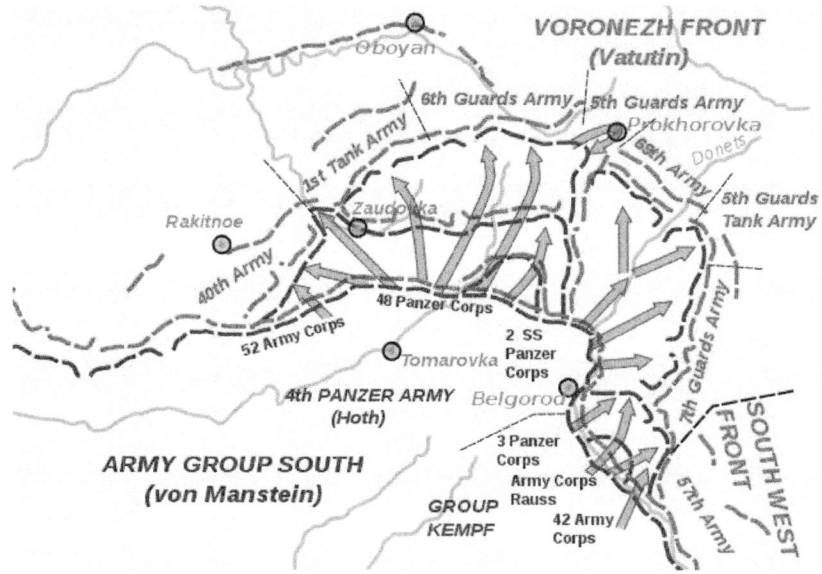

Von Manstein's corps dispositions on the eve of the battle. At the top right is the railway station town of Prokhorovka.[13]

As the 2nd SS Panzer Corps forced its way into the Soviet defensive positions, Army Detachment Kempf, which was southeast of the SS divisions and, therefore, had farther to travel, struggled to keep pace. In the early hours of July 8th, 1943, Soviet bombers knocked down a crucial bridge being built by the 3rd Panzer Division. Rather than being able to focus on pushing forward, the SS Corps was constantly having to detach units to screen and protect its eastern flanks.

The 4th Panzer Army struggled to maintain momentum amidst heavy and skillful Soviet resistance. Russian counterattacks were frequent and

---

[i] Glantz, D., and House, J., *The Battle of Kursk*, (University Press of Kansas: Kansas, 1999), p.109.

continually undermined German plans to coordinate northward attacks. For the Germans, this was what Glantz and House describe as the "Crisis in the South" over the days of July 7th to July 8th.[i] The Luftwaffe was at maximum effort and had lost a hundred aircraft. The offensive, which had initially envisaged a rapid "blitzkrieg" breakthrough of dozens of miles, was faltering.

The battle situation was always fluid and fast moving. Even as SS panzer units were making forward progress—in some cases advancing several critical miles—unhelpful distractions caused the local commanders to look over their shoulders and worry about their flanks.

"The infantry of both the [Leibstandarte and Das Reich] divisions, left behind by the advance, encountered difficulties ... attacked by strong forces of Soviet motorized infantry and about 100 tanks ... Soviet tanks broke through the German defences and nearly overran the division supply point. The panzer regiment of Das Reich Division was ordered to turn and attack the Soviets from the north. During the afternoon there were attacks at Teterevino, North Luchki and Kalinin. In one of these attacks, twenty Soviet tanks broke through and dispersed the divisional artillery ... To meet the simultaneous heavy attacks from the northwest, the northeast, and the east, the II SS Panzer Corps had to use all its reserves."[ii]

To panzer and panzergrenadier soldiers and commanders who were accustomed to advancing hundreds of miles in 1941 and 1942 during Operations Barbarossa and Blue, Operation Citadel was clearly underachieving and "woefully behind schedule."[iii]

Strenuous efforts were made to get the 2nd SS Panzer Corps' advance back on track. The 3rd SS Panzergrenadier Division relocated from the east flank to the west flank of the corps, allowing it to begin pushing north. Large-scale but poorly coordinated Soviet tank attacks were thrown in at this time. The Soviets met intense and coordinated German anti-tank fire. The attacks were driven off at a high cost for the Soviets,

---

[i] Glantz, D., and House, J., *The Battle of Kursk*, (University Press of Kansas: Kansas, 1999), p.121.

[ii] Remson, A., and Anderson, D., 'Mine and Countermine Operations in the battle of Kursk, 25 Apr. 2000, p.80.

[iii] Glantz, D., and House, J., *The Battle of Kursk*, (University Press of Kansas: Kansas, 1999), p.113.

who lost fifty tanks to ground fire and many more to the Henschel HS-129 ground attack aircraft. By the end of July 8th, the 1st SS Leibstandarte Panzergrenadier Division claimed to have destroyed over 80 Soviet tanks, and the 2nd SS Panzer Corps recorded a total of 121 Soviet tanks knocked out, losing only 17 tanks itself (although many more were damaged and in various states of disrepair).[i]

The Soviets brought up significant reinforcements over the night of July 8th. By then, the 5th Guards Tank Army, which had around six hundred tanks, was close to the front, about six miles north of Prokhorovka. It presented a serious threat to the flanks of the 2nd SS Panzer Corps.

The fighting continued on July 9th. The Luftwaffe managed 1,500 sorties that day—twice as many as the Soviets. Both sides attempted to launch their own attacks while anticipating likely enemy attacks. From the Soviet perspective, the defenses in front of Oboyan looked relatively stable even as the 2nd SS Panzer Corps attempted to refocus on the northerly direction. The 2nd Das Reich Panzergrenadier Division was protecting the right flank of the corps, southwest of Prokhorovka, and receiving Soviet armored attacks of up to eighty to one hundred tanks at a time. The fighting was intense, and the losses were high. The Germans made no significant progress toward Oboyan.[ii]

Hoth's "Fateful Order"

At the 4th Panzer Army headquarters, General Hermann Hoth was following the situation closely. There was no positive spin he could put on this. Ideally, Army Detachment Kempf should have been pushing up to the eastern flank to take the pressure off the 2nd SS Panzer Corps and allow it to drive northward. He needed Kempf to intercept and, ideally, defeat the 5th Guards Tank Army. Kempf's forces, which were struggling with river crossings, fierce resistance, and determined counterattacks, had been unable to make the desired progress. Furthermore, to the west, the 48th Panzer Corps was also struggling, as it was constantly distracted from moving north by unrelenting Soviet counterattacks. Across the front, combat power was draining away, and the Soviets still appeared to

---

[i] Glantz, D., and House, J., *The Battle of Kursk*, (University Press of Kansas: Kansas, 1999), pp.134-135.

[ii] Remson, A., and Anderson, D., 'Mine and Countermine Operations in the battle of Kursk, 25 Apr. 2000, p.84.

have a limitless supply of reinforcements.

With options limited and time very much running out, Hoth changed his plans. He decided that the threat presented by the large Soviet forces from the east was too great to be ignored. He decided to throw the 2nd SS Panzer Corps northeast toward Prokhorovka to defeat this force before it was ready to attack. If he could do that, then maybe Model would be able to move out of the northern flank of the Kursk bulge.[i]

It was a calculated risk. Hoth asked for maximum Luftwaffe support for this drive.

"The cream of von Manstein's panzer force was moving in a new direction, toward a head-to-head collision with the 5th Guards Tank Army at Prokhorovka."[ii]

Approach to a Battle

Hoth's roll of the dice got off to a problematic start. On July 10th, news broke from the Mediterranean that American and British amphibious forces had landed on the southern and eastern coastline of Sicily in what looked like the first stage of an assault on "the soft underbelly of Europe."[iii] The invasion did not come as a surprise to Hitler and his generals; they had been worrying about it ever since over a quarter of a million German and Italian soldiers surrendered in Tunisia in May. However, it did cause Hitler to look anxiously over his shoulder at a critical moment during Kursk. Germany, with its location square in the center of Europe, always feared a two-front war, which was what it had experienced in the First World War. The Germans did not want to be surrounded with its resources and reserves stretched in all directions. But now, a two-front war in Europe had arrived. It looked likely that more troops and tanks would soon be needed to support or, more realistically, take the place of the crumbling Italian Army.

On July 11th, the German forces made very few gains. The 48th Panzer Corps fought hard but to no avail. Heavy rain showers turned the tracks into mud and dry ravines into fast-flowing streams. In some areas, only

---

[i] Glantz, D., and House, J., *The Battle of Kursk*, (University Press of Kansas: Kansas, 1999), p.146.

[ii] Glantz, D., and House, J., *The Battle of Kursk*, (University Press of Kansas: Kansas, 1999), p.147.

[iii] The expression was attributed to Winston Churchill and was used to refer to Italy during the Second World War as a vulnerable and weakened power.

tracked vehicles could operate. This meant some Luftwaffe aircraft could not take off, and the truck convoys needed to provide ammunition for the German guns were hampered.

Surveying the situation, Nikolai Vatutin believed the defensive efforts of his soldiers had gone well. He was planning a large counterattack on July 12th, in which the Soviet 5th Guards Tank Army was to play a big part. However, Vatutin was acutely aware of the risk posed by the approaching 2nd SS Panzer Corps to the southwest of Prokhorovka and Army Detachment Kempf to the south of the town. By the end of July 11th, the 1st Leibstandarte Division had captured an anti-tank ditch and a wooded area on either side of the railway and road leading to Prokhorovka. They held three of the key bits of high ground and stood at the base of the final hill, Hill 252.2, that led to Prokhorovka, placing them only a couple of miles from the town's outskirts. This advance was faster than the Soviets had expected.

General Rotmistrov, the commander of the 5th Guards Tank Army, was ordered to bring his forces up quickly and be ready for rapid action. Rotmistrov prepared the orders for his tank army. However, as he conducted a reconnaissance of the likely battle area, southwest of Prokhorovka, he saw to his dismay that elements of the 2nd SS Panzer Corps had already reached the line from where Rotmistrov had been planning to launch his forces. The Germans had some crucial high ground. This required a hasty rewrite of his orders.

But things were to get even more difficult for Rotmistrov and his plans. To his consternation, he found out at about four on the morning of July 12th that there was a breakthrough at Rzhavets by the 6th Panzer Division of Kempf's 3rd Panzer Corps, about twelve miles directly south of Prokhorovka. This potentially significant breach of the Soviet lines threatened to take the Germans southeast of Prokhorovka and into the rear of the 5th Guards Tank Army. One battle group from the 6th Panzer Division had made its way under cover of dark through Rzhavets using a captured T-34 to fool the Soviet troops. In the confusion, a footbridge over the river was left intact, and the German troops slipped across the water by daybreak. More German mechanized units rushed to assist and exploit the breakthrough.[i]

---

[i] Beevor, A., *The Second World War*, (Weidenfeld and Nicolson: London, 2012), p.481.

Vatutin urgently needed this gap blocked off. He contacted Rotmistrov and ordered him to send a portion of his force farther south to intercept the panzers of the 3rd Panzer Corps. Once again, Rotmistrov had to rethink and rewrite his orders and reassign a sizable chunk of his troops. Elements of his 5th Guards Mechanized Corps and 2nd Tank Corps (approximately 150 tanks in total) were directed 10 miles south, away from Prokhorovka.

By the evening of July 11th and the early morning of July 12th, it was looking extremely likely that there would be a significant armored clash in the Prokhorovka area. Hoth was looking to continue an aggressive armored push northeast with the 1st Leibstandarte and 2nd Das Reich panzer divisions. He was hoping that the 48th Panzer Corps to his west would have some success and be able to wheel eastward to support the 2nd SS Panzer Corps. Army Detachment Kempf was pushing forward southeast of the SS panzers. The 3rd SS Totenkopf Division on the western flank of the SS troops was bogged down in heavy fighting, trying to secure a bridgehead across the Psel River and Hill 226.6 beyond it. It would play no significant part in the Prokhorovka confrontation.

From the Soviet perspective, the 5th Guards Tank Army was planning to launch its own major counterattack at more or less the same time. This was part of a broader set of Soviet attacks that also included a southward thrust by the 6th Guards Army, the 1st Tank Army, and the 5th Guards Army, and also by the 69th Army, eight miles south of Prokhorovka. These operations spanned an area of over two hundred square miles.

The Prokhorovka Battlefield

The main action would be a dramatic confrontation between the 2nd SS Panzer Corps and the 5th Guards Tank Army. It was to become known as the Battle of Prokhorovka, and it took place in an area of approximately eight miles by six miles. It was a complex battlefield, not a flat, open plain. There was rolling terrain and high ground that sometimes allowed a good field of fire and sometimes obscured the visibility of the battlefield. Hamlets and villages dotted the plains. Ravines and gullies disrupted the battlefield, providing natural obstacles that hampered movement and visibility. Tree lines, woods, orchards, and copses also hindered visibility. In addition, manmade defenses, such as anti-tank ditches and mines, restricted movement. The battlefield was bounded on the left flank by the Psel River and on the right by the railway line, which headed northeast into and beyond Prokhorovka. In many places, the railway was elevated on an embankment, making it impassable for tanks.

The 1st SS Leibstandarte Division had taken Hill 258.2, about seven miles southwest of Prokhorovka. There were at least three other significant pieces of high ground in the way before they came to the town. The Germans would have to traverse the downward slope from Hill 258.2 and then slowly climb to a higher piece of terrain, Hill 252.2, which overlooked Prokhorovka just two miles from the town. A Soviet parachute division, the 9th Guards Airborne, was dug in on a two-mile front around the western and southwestern outskirts of the town.

The number of tanks facing each other at Prokhorovka has been swept up into the myth of the battle, which is known as the greatest tank battle of all time. Post-WW2 reports, writings, and histories picked up the claim by Rotmistrov that a total of 1,500 Russian and German tanks fought it out. More recent analysis—most notably by the Russian historian Valeriy Zamulin, has strongly challenged this figure. In an article written by Zamulin entitled "Prokhorovka: Evolution of a Myth," he gives his assessment of the approximate number of tanks and self-propelled guns available to the 5th Guards Tank Army and the 2nd SS Panzer Corps.[i]

Zamulin believes that on July 11th, on the eve of the battle, the 2nd SS Panzer Corps (comprising three divisions) had 300 operational armored vehicles: 240 tanks and 60 self-propelled guns. But remember, this was for the corps as a whole. One hundred and twenty of these armored vehicles belonged to the 3rd Totenkopf Panzergrenadier Division, which was conducting operations farther west against the 5th Guards Army (as opposed to 5th Guards Tank Army), and most of these did not see action at Prokhorovka. Zamulin calculates that perhaps thirty Totenkopf tanks might have been directly involved.

Zamulin believes that 210 German tanks and self-propelled guns were available to the Germans. The 5th Guards Tank Army could muster significantly more than that: the 18th Tank Corps (150 tanks and self-propelled guns), the 29th Tank Corps (220 tanks and self-propelled guns), the 2nd Tank Corps (52 tanks and self-propelled guns; this corps had

---

[i] Zamulin, V., *The Battle of Kursk: Controversial and Neglected Aspects*, (Helion and Company: Warwick, 2022).

suffered in fighting already and had been recently attached to the 5th Guards Tank Army), and the 2nd Guards Tank Corps (100 tanks and self-propelled guns). So, it was 210 German armored vehicles against about 510 Soviet vehicles. Ten to fifteen miles farther south, where Rotmistrov had sent forces to block Kempf's potential breakthrough, around 150 Soviet armored vehicles challenged 120 German vehicles. This confrontation is generally not considered to be a part of the battle for Prokhorovka.

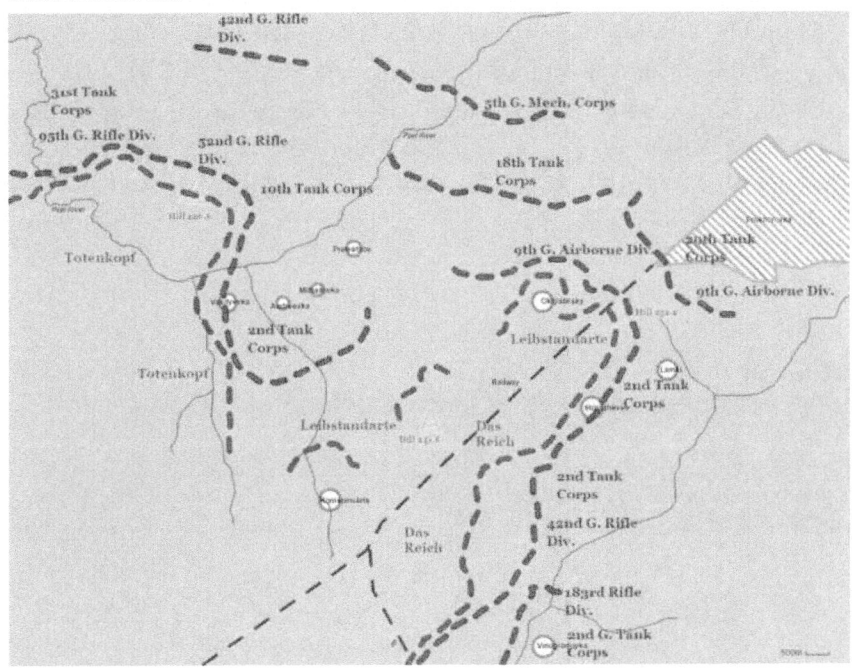

The situation on July 11th, on the eve of the Battle of Prokhorovka.[14]

At dawn on July 12th, the 2nd SS Panzer Corps began moving northeast. From reconnaissance reports, by eight in the morning, it was becoming very clear that a major Soviet armored force was heading their way. This was Rotmistrov's 5th Guards Tank Army. If Rotmistrov had instilled anything into his tank commanders for operation, it was to be aware of the serious threat that the heavily armed and armored Tiger tanks presented. The only tactic he offered was to close on the Tigers as rapidly as possible to shorten the range. This would also have the benefit of complicating the job of the German artillery and air support, as they would struggle to identify targets. This likely explains why many of the Soviet attacks that day reportedly took the form of almost suicidal charges. The Soviets did not know that only four operational Tiger tanks were facing them that day. No Panthers or Elefants were involved in the battle either.

The Soviet armored corps was hidden from the Germans' view behind rolling higher ground. Soviet aircraft and artillery launched a brief attack. Rotmistrov monitored the advancing German forces and then issued the order for his troops to conduct an all-out attack: "Steel, Steel, Steel." The 29th Tank Corps moved rapidly down the road from Prokhorovka, with the 18th Tank Corps advancing on its right. The rising sun was behind the tanks, hampering German visibility.

One of the tank commanders in the 1st SS Panzer Regiment was Rudolf von Ribbentrop. He was the son of Germany's foreign minister, Joachim von Ribbentrop. He commanded the 6th Panzer Company, equipped with Mark IV tanks. His shorthanded company had only seven tanks in total at this point.[i]

A German Mark IV tank in Russia. From 1943 onward, many Mark IVs were fitted with additional thin plates of armor on the hull and turret for added protection. This made the tank look more "box-like" and often caused enemy gunners, in the heat of battle, to mistake the vehicle for a Tiger tank.[15]

Rudolf von Ribbentrop was in an advanced position when the Soviet attack began and provided a highly credible eyewitness account. At that

---

[i] A theoretical full-strength German medium tank company in 1943 should have had twenty-two tanks. https://dupuyinstitute.org/2018/09/19/panzer-battalions-in-lssah-in-july-1943/

point in time, the SS had outposts or reconnaissance units on or around Hill 252.2. These troops had seen a large tank force approaching and fired volleys of violet-colored flares into the air, along the slope, and as far as the railway line, indicating an incoming tank attack. Von Ribbentrop's seven Mark IVs drove up the western slope of Hill 252.2 to investigate.

"On reaching the crest of the slope we saw another low rise about 200 metres away on the other side of a small valley, on which our infantry positions were obviously located ... as we drove down the forward slope we spotted the first T-34s which were apparently trying to outflank us from the left. We halted on the slope and opened fire, hitting several of the enemy. A number of Russian tanks were left burning. For a good gunner 800 metres was the ideal range."[i]

Then, the situation began to deteriorate quicker than von Ribbentrop could have expected, as the bulk of the 29th Tank Corps burst across the area.

"What I saw left me speechless. From beyond the shallow rise about 150-200 metres in front of me appeared fifteen, then thirty, then forty tanks. Finally there were too many to count. The T-34s were rolling towards us at high speed, carrying mounted infantry."[ii]

Suddenly, German and Soviet armored vehicles intermingled. Von Ribbentrop's company of seven tanks was quickly reduced to three. Tank combat took place at extremely short range, sometimes a matter of dozens of yards. The dust thrown up by frantically spinning tank tracks mingled with the black and white smoke from burning vehicles that drifted across the battlefield, compounding the chaos.

"We found ourselves taking on a seemingly inexhaustible mass of enemy armor—never have I received such an overwhelming impression of Russian strength and numbers as on that day. The clouds of dust made it difficult to get help from the Luftwaffe, and soon many of the T-34s had broken past our screen and were streaming like rats all over the old battlefield."[iii]

---

[i] Wheatley, B., *The Panzers of Prokhorovka*, (Osprey Publishing: Oxford, 2023), p.96.

[ii] Beevor, A., *The Second World War*, (Weidenfeld and Nicolson: London, 2012), p.482.

[iii] Caidin, M., *The Tigers Are Burning*, (Pinnacle Books, Los Angeles, 1980), p.237.

Command and control broke down on both sides. However, the precarious situation for the Germans was suddenly reversed. British historian Ben Wheatley carefully researched the battle and the battlefield. The Germans took control of an anti-tank ditch dug by the Soviets at the base of Hill 252.2. The mass of the 29th Corps armored vehicles was rapidly advancing toward the hill, hell-bent on closing the distance with the feared Tiger tanks. The planners of the 5th Guards Tank Army's operation (remember, the orders had been hastily rewritten twice) had either neglected the ditch or were entirely unaware of it. The Soviet tanks, moving at top speed, only recognized the obstacle for what it was when they were more or less on top of it. The attack crumbled.[i]

The plight of the Soviet tanks got worse. They stopped and attempted to find a way to right and left. All the German tanks on the other side of the ditch had to do was pick a target and shoot. Von Ribbentrop said, "Now the T-34s recognized the ditch and tried to veer left to the road, in order to get across the ditch via the bridge, which had been repaired. What happened next is indescribable ... as they converged on the bridge; the Russians were exposed on the flanks and made easier targets. Burning T-34s ran into and over each other. An inferno of fire, smoke, burning tanks, dead and wounded!"[ii]

The western slope of Hill 252.2 was covered in burning tank hulks. Over one hundred tanks of the 29th Tank Corps—nearly half of the tank force—had been destroyed in a few hours of fighting. According to Wheatley, the Germans had lost only four tanks in the same action. Reportedly, General Hausser, the commander of the 2nd SS Panzer Corps, came to the front to personally witness the scale of the Soviet losses for himself, as it was so difficult to believe.

The 18th Tank Corps, which was advancing on the right of the 29th Tank Corps, fared little better. It punched a bigger hole in the German lines, having found the gap between the Leibstandarte and Totenkopf Divisions. Large groups of T-34s breached the Germans' first line of defense. Leibstandarte sent its one Tiger tank company (of only four Tiger tanks) to deal with this breakthrough.[iii] After three hours of fighting

---

[i] Wheatley, B., *The Panzers of Prokhorovka*, (Osprey Publishing: Oxford, 2023), pp.96-97.

[ii] Wheatley, B., *The Panzers of Prokhorovka*, (Osprey Publishing: Oxford, 2023), p.97.

[iii] Out of interest, this Tiger company was commanded by Michael Wittman, who would find

and the loss of one Tiger, the 18th Tank Corps was repulsed, losing fifty-five tanks out of the nearly two hundred it had started with.

The 5th Guards Tank Army had taken a very serious beating and had inflicted little serious damage to the 2nd SS Panzer Corps. Fighting continued across the battlefield. SS light self-propelled "Marder" guns ambushed the Soviet 25th Tank Brigade of the 29th Tank Corps by the railway line and inflicted more serious losses to the Soviets. Farther south, in a sector defended by the Das Reich Division, assaults by the Soviet 2nd Tank Corps and 2nd Guards Tank Corps made no forward progress. On the left flank of the 2nd SS Panzer Corps, the Totenkopf Division, having fought off Soviet attacks during the morning, launched its own successful attack and moved forward about three miles, managing to reach a road linking Prokhorovka to Oboyan. This was to be the northernmost point reached by the 4th Panzer Army during the entire Battle of Kursk.[i]

As evening drew on, the battles began to die down out of their own accord amidst the dwindling light. The smoke and dust made it difficult to understand what was going on. Then, heavy rain began to fall. Both sides were exhausted, and neither side was entirely clear what had just happened. However, reports from troops on the ground were rapidly being sent back to higher commands on both sides. It was soon clear that the 5th Guards Tank Army had suffered severe casualties—half its armored force and thousands of soldiers. Of nearly 600 armored vehicles fielded by the 5th Guards Tank Army on July 11th, Wheatley calculates only 320 were still operational on July 16th. The wreckage of the 5th Guards Tank Army was strewn all over the battlefield.[ii]

Incredibly, of the 200 armored vehicles fielded by the 2nd SS Panzer Corps on July 11th, Wheatley records that by July 16th, the German units that had fought at Prokhorovka actually had 220 armored vehicles in their inventory. This increase in number was due to repairs, replacements, and new vehicles being fed into the line. During this phase

---

brief fame in the early days of the summer 1944 Normandy campaign, where he conducted a very successful ambush against the British 7th Armored Division at Villers Bocage on June 13th, 1944, inflicting many tank and vehicle losses. A month later, Wittman died in his Tiger tank in Normandy in another tank duel.

[i] Wheatley, B., *The Panzers of Prokhorovka*, (Osprey Publishing: Oxford, 2023), pp.103-103.

[ii] Beevor, A., *The Second World War*, (Weidenfeld and Nicolson: London, 2012), p.483.

of the Battle of Kursk, with the German units primarily pushing forward, any tank that suffered minor damage, such as broken tracks, could be recovered, taken back to a repair depot, and quickly fixed. Later, in the battles during August and September, German forces were more frequently on the retreat. Many otherwise repairable vehicles often had to be abandoned or blown up because there was no means of recovering them.

But the scoresheet of losses does not tell the whole story. Although the Soviets may well have taken the heaviest losses at Prokhorovka, they had halted the forward momentum of the SS armored formations.[i] With that, any hope that the Germans could still break through to Kursk disappeared completely. The Germans were out of options.

---

[i] Wheatley, B., *The Panzers of Prokhorovka*, (Osprey Publishing: Oxford, 2023), p.106.

Chapter 8 – Hitler Wavers, and the Soviets Counterattack

On July 13th, Adolf Hitler summoned the senior commanders of Operation Citadel back to his headquarters in East Prussia. He had decided to end the Kursk offensive. The Allies had a secure foothold in Sicily, and the Italian resistance was collapsing. More immediately critical was the powerful Soviet Operation Kutuzov, against the Germans' own salient at Orel, north of the 9th Panzer Army. This operation had commenced on July 12th. The scale of Kutuzov threatened to dwarf the entire German Kursk operation.

Hitler received little argument from his commanders. Von Kluge, the commander of Army Group Center, was in agreement. He reported that the 9th Army had stalled and was now spending most of its efforts on Kutuzov to the east. Von Manstein, however, argued for more time to develop his operations in the south, believing that he had more or less breached the last Soviet defensive line (there were, in fact, three more). He thought he could inflict further damage on the Soviets. Hitler gave him a few more days.[i]

---

[i] Remson, A., and Anderson, D., 'Mine and Countermine Operations in the battle of Kursk, 25 Apr. 2000, p. 103.

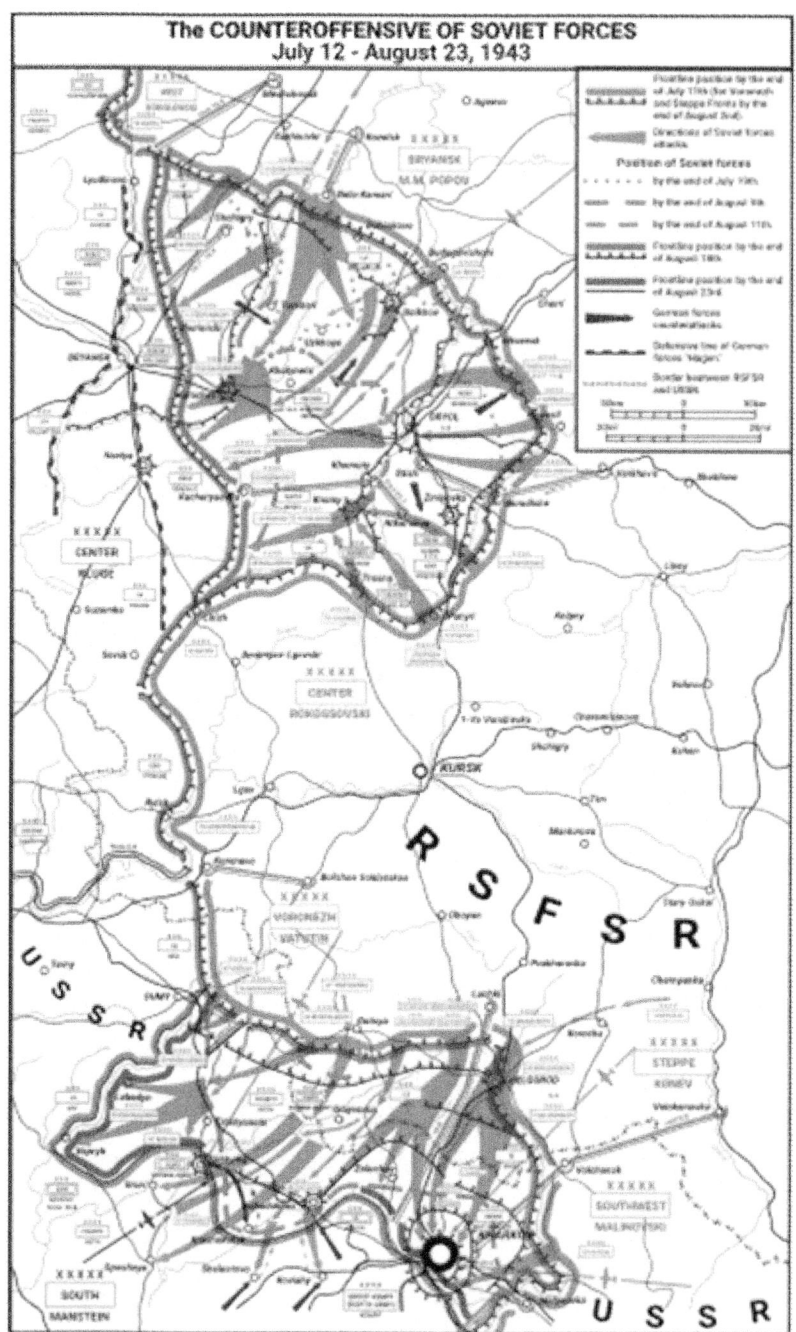

The two Soviet counteroffensives, Kutuzov (north) and Rumyantsev (south), were of a similar scale or somewhat larger than the German operations around the Kursk salient and came at a time when the Germans had expended most of their preserved armor and manpower.[16]

The final stages of the Kursk campaign were beginning. Operation Kutuzov was going well for the Soviets. The 6th Guards Army had advanced ten miles in two days. However, the Elefant detachments, which had been pulled out of the Kursk salient and sent to support the 2nd Panzer Army, did better on this front. Wider fields of fire and extended visible distances allowed them to pick off Soviet tanks at long range.

Von Manstein hurried back to the southern flank, where more fierce fighting took place, but the situation largely remained a stalemate. A small-scale operation known as Roland took place to little effect. Most of the 4th Panzer Army were very much on the defensive. The 48th Panzer Corps was assailed regularly by fresh Soviet infantry divisions.[i]

The 2nd SS Panzer Corps made a few aggressive probes toward Prokhorovka, and impressively, the 3rd Panzer Corps made some significant advances. However, this was no longer a constructive use of the dwindling German armored resources. On July 15th, Hitler stopped the Kursk operation completely. The 4th Panzer Army issued an order to its divisions that evening: "To stop the offensive and be prepared to withdraw southward to the lines held on 4th July."[ii] This must have been a bitter pill to swallow, for soldiers and generals alike.

Hoth was compelled to give up some of his best divisions. The 2nd SS Panzer Corps was pulled out of the line for a much-needed refit and to prepare for departure to Italy. The Grossdeutschland Division was sent north to help repel the Kutuzov attack.

On July 22nd, Hitler authorized Model to vacate the Orel salient. In the south, by July 23rd, the 4th Panzer Army was back where it had started on July 4th.

On August 3rd, the Soviets launched another major strategic offensive, this time against the 4th Panzer Army and Army Detachment Kempf. Operation Rumyantsev hit the 2nd SS Panzer Corps just north of Belgorod with over a million men, 2,400 tanks, and 13,000 guns. The thrust of the attack drove southwest, aiming to recapture Kharkov in the fourth major battle for the city. It was a surprise for the Germans that the

---

[i] Remson, A., and Anderson, D., 'Mine and Countermine Operations in the battle of Kursk, 25 Apr. 2000 p.103.

[ii] Remson, A., and Anderson, D., 'Mine and Countermine Operations in the battle of Kursk, 25 Apr. 2000, p.107.

Soviets could have regrouped and replaced their losses so quickly after Kursk.

"Manstein had not expected such a powerful onslaught so soon. 'For the weary German infantry, it was as if their beaten enemy had risen from the grave with renewed strength.' Two days later Belgorod was retaken, and the Red Army could now focus on Kharkov."[1]

The days of German advances in Russia were over. A long retreat was beginning. It would end in the rubble-filled streets of Berlin less than two years later.

---

[1] Beevor, A., *The Second World War*, (Weidenfeld and Nicolson: London, 2012), p.484

Chapter 9 – Aftermath

On July 12th and over the next four days of intense fighting, the 5th Guards Tank Army had lost more than half of the tanks and self-propelled guns it had committed to the battle.[i]

In the immediate aftermath of the 5th Guards Tank Army's clash at Prokhorovka, General Rotmistrov's staff got down to the business of writing up an "after action report." This was standard practice so that other commanders and the Soviet military machine, in general, could understand what had happened in the battle and what lessons could be learned to help in future battles.

However, there was another reason for the Soviets to pay close attention to the account of the battle. Within a couple of weeks, Rotmistrov was summoned to Stalin to explain why he appeared to have lost the best part of an entire tank army. Displeasing Stalin was not to be recommended. General Rokossovsky had felt the wrath of Stalin's secret police in the 1930s; it had involved illegal detention, beating, and torture, including having his teeth forcibly removed. Rotmistrov was anxious, perhaps for very understandable reasons, to give a good account, one that justified his actions, explained the losses his army had suffered, and put the battle in the best light. So, herein lies the beginning of the myth-making around the Battle of Kursk.

---

[i] Zamulin, V., *The Battle of Kursk: Controversial and Neglected Aspects*, (Helion and Company: Warwick, 2022), p.380.

"A Shining Model of Self-conceit and Elaborate Fabrications"

Rotmistrov's account was deliberately exaggerated and distorted to inflate the scale of the battle, to emphasize the decisive impact that the 5th Guards Tank Army's intervention had on the outcome of the southern salient, and, above all, to make a big claim for the amount of damage inflicted upon the 2nd SS Panzer Corps to deflect from the losses his own army had suffered. The story, which was largely accepted by the high command in the end, told of an armored clash between a combined total of 1,500 armored vehicles in which the Germans had suffered heavily. Rotmistrov's career had been on a knife's edge, but he seemed to have gotten away with it; Kursk was a victory, so it was better not to ask too many uncomfortable questions. The tagline "the greatest tank battle in the history of the Great Patriotic War" seemed to be set in stone. As the years went by, it was seen as unhelpful and career-limiting to challenge the official account.[ii]

Even so, over the years, Rotmistrov's account continued to be questioned. The size of the armored clash could not be reconciled with the facts. The 5th Guards Tank Army's intelligence officers appeared to have greatly overreported the number of German panzer divisions at Prokhorovka, claiming there were seven divisions. There were only two and a half. The Russian account even stated that divisions from the 48th Panzer Corps and the 24th Panzer Corps saw action. The 48th Panzer Corps was engaged much farther west, and the 24th Panzer Corps did not see action at all in the Battle of Kursk! Panthers and Elefants were also wrongly claimed to be present on the battlefield; the Panthers served exclusively in the Grossdeutschland Division to the west, and the Elefants only operated on the northern front under Model. If a German panzer division was identified by Soviet intelligence analysts, they automatically recorded that this meant two hundred tanks, with some "rounding down" this number if they knew the division had already been in combat for a few days. What seems more plausible, at least according to Zamulin's research, was a clash involving one thousand armored vehicles spread over an area of ten to twelve miles.

---

[i] Zamulin, V., *The Battle of Kursk: Controversial and Neglected Aspects*, (Helion and Company: Warwick, 2022), p.380.

[ii] Zamulin, V., *The Battle of Kursk: Controversial and Neglected Aspects*, (Helion and Company: Warwick, 2022), chapter 12, 'Prokhorovka – the evolution of a myth.'

Hanging over everything was the claim that around four hundred German tanks and armored vehicles had been destroyed. Where were they? The Germans did not have that many tanks in the battle. Two German panzer divisions had done the bulk of the fighting. On the day before the battle, the 1ˢᵗ SS Leibstandarte reported having 89 operational tanks and self-propelled guns, and the 2ⁿᵈ Das Reich reported having 107.[i] Neither reported any significant changes to that combat strength four days later. According to historian Ben Wheatley, Leibstandarte seems to have lost five tanks, including just one Tiger.

Many of Rotmistrov's officers were unimpressed by his self-serving claims even years later. The year 1963 was the twentieth anniversary of the Battle of Kursk, and the issue reared its head again, perhaps inflamed by a book written by Rotmistrov in 1960 that broadly repeated his claims. Some senior figures did not agree.

"Marshal of the Soviet Union G.K. Zhukov totally believed that on 12 July 1943, nothing particular happened at the [Prokhorovka] railroad station that affected the war's outcome … and called upon [Rotmistrov] to be more modest … Other generals acted more diplomatically, but weren't hiding their negative attitude toward such myth-making."[ii]

Rotmistrov appeared to recognize the difficult situation he was in. His later writings showed attempts to revise the figure of 1,500 tanks. He instead wrote there were 1,200 armored vehicles. This had limited impact. At a 1963 academic seminar, Rotmistrov was put in the spotlight and asked tough questions about the battle. Perhaps he snapped under the questioning, or perhaps he was fed up with the disrespect he had received. Perhaps he genuinely wanted to set the record straight. Here is a summary of the key points (as per Zamulin) reportedly made by Rotmistrov at the seminar in response to all the criticisms leveled at the 5ᵗʰ Guards Tank Army's performance and his own leadership on July 12ᵗʰ.[iii] You can almost sense his frustration as he finally unloads.

---

[i] Wheatley, B., *The Panzers of Prokhorovka*, (Osprey Publishing: Oxford, 2023), p.91.

[ii] Zamulin, V., *The Battle of Kursk: Controversial and Neglected Aspects*, (Helion and Company: Warwick, 2022), chapter 12, 'Prokhorovka – the evolution of a myth,' p.390.

[iii] Zamulin, V., *The Battle of Kursk: Controversial and Neglected Aspects*, (Helion and Company: Warwick, 2022), chapter 12, 'Prokhorovka – the evolution of a myth,' p.392.

1. We had no fire support from the front-level artillery. A self-propelled gun regiment and an anti-tank brigade were promised to us but did not turn up.
2. Our deployment area changed twice, and the Germans had the favorable ground.
3. The Soviet tanks were inferior.[i]
4. At least we stopped the enemy attack, even though at a high cost.
5. The high losses suffered by the 5th Guards Tank Army were his responsibility as the commander.
6. Time was short; there was no full supporting artillery barrage and no full reconnaissance. Access to intelligence reports was also limited.
7. This is why we did not manage to advance and did not smash the 2nd SS Panzer Corps, but at least we protected the gap and stopped the Germans from advancing.
8. Regarding the claims of high numbers of German tank losses, the figures were compiled from many different sub-unit reports after the battle. Often, anti-tank guns were firing at the same tank, leading to multiple claims. For each destroyed tank, there might have been three, four, or even twelve times the number of claims of a kill.[ii]

---

[i] This is an interesting and probably fair point. Although the T-34 was an excellent weapon (arguably one of the best tanks of the war), not all Rotmistrov's tanks were T-34s. About a third of the tank force comprised light Soviet T-60 or T-70 tanks, which were little more than reconnaissance vehicles.

[ii] Zamulin, V., *The Battle of Kursk: Controversial and Neglected Aspects*, (Helion and Company: Warwick, 2022), chapter 12, 'Prokhorovka – the evolution of a myth.'

Conclusion

The Battle of Kursk was undoubtedly a massive and decisive armored confrontation that ended up a significant defeat for the German Army. Perhaps the Soviet forces were careless with the lives of its men, as they engaged in counterattack after counterattack. Both sides suffered very high losses of men, tanks, aircraft, and materiel, but only one side was capable of replacing those losses.

After Kursk, the strategic initiative passed to Stalin, Stavka (the Soviet high command), and the Soviet Armed Forces. This 1943 German attempt to repeat the blitzkrieg of the previous years was highly miscalculated by a hesitant and uncertain Hitler, who was supported by insecure generals who were unwilling to put their careers on the line by telling him the truth. Perhaps Guderian was the lone exception to this (although we only have his word for it). The German soldiers had gone into battle with large amounts of confidence. In the late spring of 1943, their divisions were approaching full strength. They also believed the Soviet soldiers were weak.

It was the first (and last) time the blitzkrieg was attempted in a situation where the enemy knew the time and location of the attack and had had months to prepare for it. The Soviet forces fought bravely and tenaciously; there were no collapses in the front line, and negligible amounts of Russian prisoners were taken. The Wehrmacht would never be able to launch an assault on this scale ever again.

It is also worth remembering that the battle was not just about tank versus tank. Airpower, artillery, trenches, mines, and the weather all played important parts in the conflict. Could the Germans have won at Kursk if they had launched the attack earlier, perhaps in April or May as some had advised? It seems highly unlikely. There would certainly have been fewer Soviet defensive lines, but both sides were weakened and disorganized after the fighting of the winter. Zamulin's research shows that in May 1943, German panzer divisions desperately lacked tanks and that Soviet tank numbers outnumbered the Germans by about 1.5 to 1.[i] The Germans would have had no numerical advantage.

What if the Germans had won at Kursk? Let's remind ourselves of Guderian's reported observation to Adolf Hitler: "It's a matter of profound indifference to the world whether we hold Kursk or not. I repeat my question: Why do we want to attack in the East at all this year?"[ii]

The loss of the Kursk salient would certainly have been a setback for the Soviets, but it also would have been a setback for the Germans, assuming they suffered heavy losses grinding through six or seven defensive lines to Kursk rather than the one or two they actually managed to penetrate.

Would it have been strategically decisive in any way? The Soviet forces still had a mass of reserves to the north, south, and east that it could have thrown into the battle, perhaps at the cost of delaying or even canceling the Kutuzov and Rumyantsev offensives. The Germans would have exhausted themselves capturing a medium-sized railway and communications town in the middle of central Russia, with autumn soon to arrive.

Arguably, it would have been far more prudent for Hitler simply not to have launched Operation Citadel at all and instead fall back to defensible river lines and use Guderian's newly rebuilt panzer divisions to conduct mobile defenses of the type that von Manstein was skilled at. However, as the British historian James Holland has argued, a flexible defense on the Eastern Front might have bought the Germans another year, but it would not have won the war.[iii] And falling back was never a

---

[i] Zamulin, V., *The Battle of Kursk: Controversial and Neglected Aspects*, (Helion and Company: Warwick, 2022), chapter 12, 'Prokhorovka – the evolution of a myth,' p.127.

[ii] Glantz, D., and House, J., *The Battle of Kursk*, (University Press of Kansas: Kansas, 1999), p.3.

[iii] Holland, J., 'Battle of Kursk,' History Hit Warfare podcast, 21 Aug. 2023, https://podcasts.apple.com/us/podcast/battle-of-kursk-with-james-

favored option for Adolf Hitler.

But this is all with the benefit of hindsight. The Battle of Kursk—and the associated "what ifs"—still intrigues new generations of historians, researchers, and people who simply have a fascination for the human drama of conflict. Ben Wheatley's recent studies show there is still much more to learn about this titanic struggle. Zamulin's research gives a highly credible reworking of the myths surrounding Kursk. However, Zamulin, above all, cautions that although compelling evidence is now available for those who care to spend the time, many people, even in 2024, still default to the production of the easier myths and clichés. This is a risk for all historians.

If you enjoyed this book, a review on Amazon would be greatly appreciated because it would mean a lot to hear from you.

To leave a review:
1. Open your camera app.
2. Point your mobile device at the QR code.
3. The review page will appear in your web browser.

Thanks for your support!

Here's another book by Captivating History that you might like

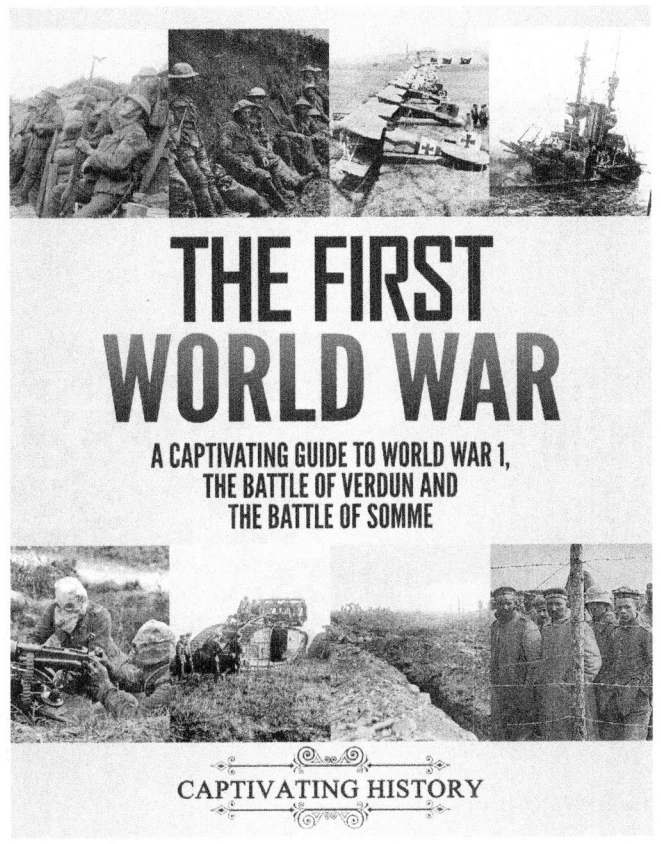

Free Bonus from Captivating History (Available for a Limited time)

Hi History Lovers!

Now you have a chance to join our exclusive history list so you can get your first history ebook for free as well as discounts and a potential to get more history books for free!

Simply visit the link below to join.

Or, Scan the QR code!

captivatinghistory.com/ebook

Also, make sure to follow us on Facebook, X, and YouTube by searching for Captivating History.

Reference

'Building the Tiger Tank,' The Tank Museum, 16 Mar. 2020, https://tankmuseum.org/article/building-a-tiger-tank/

'Fight Them on the Beaches,' International Churchill Society, website accessed 7 June 2024, https://winstonchurchill.org/resources/speeches/1940-the-finest-hour/fight-them-on-the-beaches/

'German Tanks at Kursk,' The Tank Museum, 18 July 2107, https://tankmuseum.org/article/german-tanks-kursk

'T-34 Tank,' Russia in global perspective, Website accessed 12 June 2024, https://russiaglobal.omeka.fas.harvard.edu/exhibits/show/objects/politics/t34#_edn7

A theoretical full-strength German medium tank company in 1943 should have had twenty-two tanks. https://dupuyinstitute.org/2018/09/19/panzer-battalions-in-lssah-in-july-1943/

Beevor, A., The Second World War, (Weidenfeld and Nicolson: London, 2012).

Caidin, M., The Tigers Are Burning, (Pinnacle Books, Los Angeles, 1980).

Carell, P., Hitler's War on Russia, (Harrap Ltd: London, 1987).

Eisenhower, D., Crusade in Europe, (William Heinemann Limited: London, 1949).

Glantz, D., and House, J., The Battle of Kursk, (University Press of Kansas: Kansas, 1999).

Guderian, H., Panzer Leader, (Futura: London, 1980).

Hind, C., & Nicolaides, A. (2020). Ace of Aces: Erich Hartmann the Blond Knight of Germany. Open Journal of Social Sciences, 8, 383-406.

https://doi.org/10.4236/jss.2020.83034.

Holland, J., 'Battle of Kursk,' History Hit Warfare podcast, 21 Aug. 2023, https://podcasts.apple.com/us/podcast/battle-of-kursk-with-james-holland/id1526490428?i=1000624778741

Manstein, E. von, Lost Victories, (Zenith Press: Minneapolis, 2004).

Mellenthin, F. von, Panzer Battles, (Futura Publications Ltd: London, 1979.

Murray, W., 'Strategy for Defeat: The Luftwaffe, 1933-1945,' Air University Press, Jan. 1983.

Remson, A., and Anderson, D., 'Mine and Countermine Operations in the battle of Kursk, 25 Apr. 2000.

Rudel, H., Stuka Pilot, (Ballantine Books: New York, 1958).

Sajer, G., The Forgotten Soldier, (Sphere Books Ltd: London, 1980).

Vandergriff, D., 'How the Germans Defined Auftragstaktik: What Mission Command is – and –is not,' Small Wars Journal, 21 June 2018, https://smallwarsjournal.com/jrnl/art/how-germans-defined-auftragstaktik-what-mission-command-and-not

Weal, J., Jagdgeschwader 52: The Experten, (Osprey Publishing: Oxford, 2004).

Wheatley, B., The Panzers of Prokhorovka, (Osprey Publishing: Oxford, 2023).

Zamulin, V., The Battle of Kursk: Controversial and Neglected Aspects, (Helion and Company: Warwick, 2022).

Zamulin, V., The Battle of Kursk: Controversial and Neglected Aspects, (Helion and Company: Warwick, 2022).

Zhukov, G., Reminiscences and Reflections, (Progress Publishers: Moscow, 1985).

Image Sources

[1] *Gdr at the English-language Wikipedia, CC BY-SA 3.0 <http://creativecommons.org/licenses/by-sa/3.0/>, via Wikimedia Commons; https://commons.wikimedia.org/wiki/File:Eastern_Front_1941-06_to_1941-12.png*

[2] *User:Gdr, CC BY-SA 3.0 <http://creativecommons.org/licenses/by-sa/3.0/>, via Wikimedia Commons; https://commons.wikimedia.org/wiki/File:Eastern_Front_1942-05_to_1942-11.png*

[3] *Gdr at the English-language Wikipedia, CC BY-SA 3.0 <http://creativecommons.org/licenses/by-sa/3.0/>, via Wikimedia Commons; https://commons.wikimedia.org/wiki/File:Eastern_Front_1942-11_to_1943-03.png*

[4] *Gdr at the English-language Wikipedia, CC BY-SA 3.0 <http://creativecommons.org/licenses/by-sa/3.0/>, via Wikimedia Commons; https://commons.wikimedia.org/wiki/File:Eastern_Front_1943-02_to_1943-08.png*

[5] *https://commons.wikimedia.org/wiki/File:Walther_Model_on_the_front_(2).jpg*

[6] *RIA Novosti archive, image #4408 / N. Bode / CC-BY-SA 3.0, CC BY-SA 3.0 <https://creativecommons.org/licenses/by-sa/3.0>, via Wikimedia Commons; https://commons.wikimedia.org/wiki/File:RIAN_archive_4408_Armor_piercers_on_the_Kursk_Bulge.jpg*

[7] *https://commons.wikimedia.org/wiki/File:Operation_Kutusov_(map).jpg*

[8] *https://commons.wikimedia.org/wiki/File:Kursk_south.svg*

[9] *https://commons.wikimedia.org/wiki/File:SU-122_4._TA_1943.jpg*

[10] *Bundesarchiv, Bild 101I-655-5976-04 / Grosse / CC-BY-SA 3.0, CC BY-SA 3.0 DE <https://creativecommons.org/licenses/by-sa/3.0/de/deed.en>, via Wikimedia Commons; https://commons.wikimedia.org/wiki/File:Bundesarchiv_Bild_101I-655-5976-04,_Russland,_Sturzkampfbomber_Junkers_Ju_87_G.jpg*

[11] *https://commons.wikimedia.org/wiki/File:Henschel_Hs_129B.jpg*

[12] *Bundesarchiv, Bild 183-J14778 / CC-BY-SA 3.0, CC BY-SA 3.0 DE <https://creativecommons.org/licenses/by-sa/3.0/de/deed.en>, via Wikimedia Commons; https://commons.wikimedia.org/wiki/File:Bundesarchiv_Bild_183-J14778,_Russland,_Grenadiere_auf_Sturmgesch%C3%BCtz.jpg*

[13] *https://commons.wikimedia.org/wiki/File:Kursk_south.svg*

[14] *EyeTruth at English Wikipedia, CC BY-SA 3.0 <https://creativecommons.org/licenses/by-sa/3.0>, via Wikimedia Commons; https://commons.wikimedia.org/wiki/File:Prokhorovka,_Battle_of_Kursk,_night_11_July.png*

[15] *Bundesarchiv, Bild 101I-088-3734A-19A / Schönemann / CC-BY-SA 3.0, CC BY-SA 3.0 DE <https://creativecommons.org/licenses/by-sa/3.0/de/deed.en>, via Wikimedia Commons; https://commons.wikimedia.org/wiki/File:Bundesarchiv_Bild_101I-088-3734A-19A,_Russland,_Panzer_IV.jpg*

[16] *Dymetrios, CC BY-SA 4.0 <https://creativecommons.org/licenses/by-sa/4.0>, via Wikimedia Commons; https://commons.wikimedia.org/wiki/File:The_COUNTEROFFENSIVE_OF_SOVIET_FORCES_July_12_-_August_23,_1943_EN.svg*

Printed in Great Britain
by Amazon